BREXIT
KBO

Jonathan S. Swift

Senior Lecturer in International
Business & Marketing

Salford Business School
University of Salford
Manchester M5 4WT

Dedication

To all those people who voted 'leave', do not believe the embittered 'remainers' who tell you that you were mislead, that the situation is too complex for you to understand, that you did not know what you were voting for.

The only difficulties are those made by the remainers themselves, who have still not accepted the outcome of a democratic referendum. Their constant undermining of the result does nothing to help the UK negotiators: in effect they are more akin to a 'Fifth Column' acting on behalf of Brussels, as they are of immense psychological help to the EU in its desperate fight to ensure that we do not leave.

However, as it cannot prevent us from leaving, then – as the EU leadership has spitefully demonstrated in its 'negotiations' in the first year of the two-year negotiating period – it is determined to punish us to deter other nations from following in our footsteps (Johnston, 2017:14).

As the ex-President of France, François Holland, is reported to have said about the UK vote to leave: "There must be a threat, there must be a risk, there must be a price, otherwise we will be in negotiations that will not end well..." (Foster and Day, 2016: 18).

Our only defence against this unelected, corrupt, vindictive monolith is to carry on regardless, and not be diverted from the path demanded by the majority.

My thanks to
Sir William Cash, MP, for writing the 'Foreword' to this book.

Thanks also to
Adrian and Neil for comments on the draft.
Debbie and Sarah for ideas on the graphics.

This does not necessarily mean that they agree with the views expressed in this book.

– Jonathan S. Swift

ISBN 1-903-499-94-1
978-1-903499-94-8

Printed and bound in the United Kingdom by 4edge Ltd, 7a Eldon Way Industrial Estate, Hockley, Essex, SS5 4AD.

FSC
www.fsc.org
FSC® C102342

The mark of
responsible forestry

Contents

BREXIT: KBO*

"This fortress built by Nature for herself
Against infection and the hand of war,
This happy breed of men, this little world,
This precious stone set in the silver sea,
Which serves it in the office of a wall
Or as a moat defensive to a house,
Against the envy of less happier lands,
This blessed plot, this earth, this realm, this England."

– *Richard II* (William Shakespeare)

*KBO ("keep buggering on") was a famous saying of Sir Winston Churchill, Prime Minister of the UK during World War 2, and was used when the country stood alone, and the threat from Nazi invasion was at its height. Basically, it meant 'carry on regardless', but was typically couched in more colourful Churchillian prose.

Foreword

This short book achieves a major objective, which is to encapsulate in a relatively short compass of 150-odd pages an admirable summary of why we had to leave the European Union, and why the British people voted to do so on 23 June 2016.

This vote was achieved over a much longer timespan than the Referendum Campaign itself. It was finally realised because – through tenacity and a sense of purpose – Parliamentarians in particular, by rebellion from the Maastricht Treaty onwards, combined with persistent calls for a referendum, succeeded in their quest.

The Maastricht Referendum Campaign was devised to bypass collusion between the Labour and Conservative frontbenchers to stay in the European Union. Jonathan Swift identifies the essential elements why 'KBO' in Churchill's own celebrated acronym was the only way to win. I strongly commend the book to those who want a short but effective summary of how it all happened, but with one caveat – we have to KBO for some time yet before the victory is complete!

Sir Bill Cash
Member of Parliament for Stone

Introduction

Why is this book necessary? It was written to reinforce the "Brexit" message to an increasingly weary and sceptical UK public, led along the road to scepticism by a group of people who were amazed at the result of the European Union (EU) referendum, who do not want us to leave the EU, and will apparently do whatever they can to frustrate the outcome of a democratic vote. Throughout the campaign they tried many ways – including a series of threats dressed up as 'facts' – to persuade people to vote to stay: this was commonly known as 'Project Fear', and showed people in privileged positions trying to use their presumed superior knowledge to their personal advantage.

By contrast, as a *Daily Telegraph* editorial pointed out "...Brexit is a reassertion of self-government that could, if exploited correctly, make Britain even richer. The case for it needs to be made over and over again." (Editorial, 2017e:17). Reinforcing the case for Brexit and ensuring that what was promised actually happens, and by the date at which it should happen, is the key objective of this book.

The book makes no claim to be impartial. It will not present a 'balanced' argument, as the author contends that those who voted for Brexit are in need of support for their position: despite the outcome of the democratic referendum, many 'remain' supporters continue to try to sabotage the exit process, and to do this they have a plethora of highly-influential individuals and institutions to argue their case.

In June 2015, a year before the referendum, David Cameron ensured a boost in support for the 'remain' campaign when he lifted the ban on the government and the European Commission spending "...millions of pounds of taxpayer's money..." (Shipman, 2015a:1) on trying to persuade people to vote to stay in the EU: similar help was not available for those who advocated 'leave.'

Further financial support was provided during the campaign, when the investment bank Goldman Sachs reportedly donated a 'substantial' six-figure sum to the 'remain' campaign in January 2016 (Dominiczak and Swinford, 2016:4), and it was reported that Lord Sainsbury gave £2.9-million to "...five different campaign groups in the run-up to the EU referendum ..." (Maidment, 2018:4), all of which were lobbying for a 'remain' vote.

In April 2016, just two months before the vote, the government spent an estimated £9-million on sending what were described as 'information' leaflets to every household, urging voters to back 'remain.' James Landale, the BBC's Deputy Political Editor, commented that the pamphlet was "...official-looking, containing pictures of workers, shoppers and families, and concentrating overwhelmingly on what the government sees as the economic case for staying in the EU. It claims that 'over three million UK jobs are linked to exports to the

EU' and that 'if the UK voted to leave the EU, the resulting economic shock would risk higher prices of some household goods'" (Landale, 2016). However, despite this and other attempts at influencing the vote, 'leave' still won; one cannot help but question what the 'leave' majority might have been had voters not been subjected to such tactics, and to the associated threats from 'Project Fear' (see chapter 2).

That there are relatively fewer figures and institutions prepared to stand up for Brexit should come as no surprise – after all, for years the EU has supported a self-serving, highly-paid Brussels elite who are in danger of losing their cushioned life-style, and will fight by any and all means possible to preserve the *status quo*. Their message has been relayed by a similar group of like-minded vested interests in the UK, many of whom have personally benefited from the UK's EU membership – people such as Neil Kinnock (BBC, 2016c), ex-EU Commissioner for Transport (appointed 1995), and who according to *The Times* (Zeffman, 2016:10), receives an estimated £60,000 annual pension from the EU, in addition to a one-off payment of nearly £273,000 on leaving office in 2004.[1]

Industry also has its 'remain' cheerleaders, as the globalisation of economies through EU membership has been of great financial benefit to major international commercial organisations, and as these organisations prosper, so to do their senior managers and shareholders – thus explaining the largely negative attitude towards Brexit by many major international corporations.

The public must not be bullied into accepting that Brexit was a 'mistake' and/or is impossible to deliver; there is growing evidence that many of those who voted 'remain' do not respect the democratic outcome, and will try to frustrate the process at every available opportunity – the most obvious tactic being to convince the British public that Brexit is just too difficult and complex to deliver in a manner that will ensure the future prosperity of the UK. However, as Charles Moore recently observed, rather than focus on negotiation minutiae and problems, we should be looking at the larger picture and political will. Comparing Brexit with the process the UK went through to join the EEC back in the early 1970s, Moore pointed out that:

"When we negotiated to join the European Community, there were innumerable intricacies which needed working out (and sometimes, as with fishing, were worked out very badly). But none of these could ultimately stop us joining, which depended not on detail, but on desire... it is in the interests of those who do not wish us to leave to insist that it is so mind-blowingly complicated that they must be put in charge of it" (Moore, 2017:18).

Although the majority voted to leave, it appears we have nearly one more year of wrangling before we can put into effect what the majority wanted.[2] During

---

1. On leaving office, Kinnock was reportedly earning £163,453 a year (Zeffman, 2016).
2. The arguments have already begun, with the High Court ruling in 2016 that the government cannot trigger Article 50 without 'consulting' parliament.

the remainder of the two-year period (from the triggering of Article 50 to actual departure), there will be an intensification of the continual drip-feed of 'information', advice, and threats from those who wanted us to remain in the EU. They are well-supported and organised, as they have the full power of the Brussels machinery, major international organisations (such as the IMF), many UK businesses, and 'authoritative' figures to champion their cause – people such as Sir John Major, and Tony Blair – although in the latter case, anything that this former Prime Minister may say is likely to be counter-productive, as he is still regarded as highly toxic due to his involvement in the Iraq War (Hennessy, 2012; Nineham, 2014).

Added to this is the intransigence of the EU negotiating team, headed by Michel Barnier, who was criticised in the UK press for an "...ill-judged and unhelpful attack on the UK." He also created tension between the EU and UK negotiators by writing an article in the French newspaper *Le Monde*, in which "...he claimed Britain would be less secure after Brexit..." (Crisp et. al., 2017:1). Why Barnier should be so concerned about the future well-being of the UK is a mystery, as this has never apparently troubled him before; one is forced to ask whether this concern for the UK is genuine, or whether it masks a much greater concern for the economic and political well-being of the EU following our departure?

Those who voted to leave the EU are fast becoming disillusioned with the apparent lethargy with which the government is approaching 'negotiations', the reported attempts to sabotage the process by British civil servants (Swinford, 2017d: 1), and the unhelpful comments in public by the current Chancellor of the Exchequer, Philip Hammond and lesser politicians such as Tim Fallon, the ex-leader of the Leader of the Liberal Democrats. There is a danger that if the 'remainers' (commonly referred to as 'remoaners') continue with their briefings and threats, calls for a second referendum, and attempts to undermine the negotiating position of the government, then Brexit will fail, and the powerful vested interests (both in the UK and abroad) will have been able to overturn a democratic vote.

The reasons why people voted 'leave' should, therefore, be reinforced before we are forced to go 'cap in hand' back to Brussels and beg to be re-admitted. Jean-Claude Juncker, President of the European Commission[3] has already publicly expressed his preference for the UK to be 're-admitted' at some unspecified time in the future (Boffey and Rankin, 2017).

Were this to happen, apart from the national shame and ignominy it would cause, the EU elites – such as Juncker, who is an arch-EU Federalist and no friend of the UK – would undoubtedly insist on our re-admission being on considerably

---

3. *The* key EU position, decided by the European Heads of State, and their choice is approved by European Parliament; the President of the Commission is *not* elected by popular vote from amongst the citizens of the EU member states.

less favourable terms than we have at the moment. David Smith, writing in *The Sunday Times* suggested, that if people are "...walking towards a very deep hole, it would be remiss not to warn them" (Smith, 2016:4); although he was using this simile to explain why his pre-referendum column was unashamedly pro-remain, the logic serves either side equally well. We cannot, therefore, afford to slow (let alone reverse) the Brexit momentum.

Guy Platten, Chief Executive of the UK Chamber of Shipping holds the media partly responsible for the consistently anti-Brexit message, as there appears to be dual standards for coverage of Brexit-related news:

"When BMW announced that their new model of the Mini was to be built in Oxford, for example, or that Amazon and Google have made fresh (and huge) investments in the UK, or that London has extended its lead as the world's top financial centre, the coverage in pro-remain publications was scant, or the news was dismissed as an anomaly in an atmosphere of wider economic misery. Yet when Lloyd's of London announced that "tens" of jobs were to be moved to a European office, it dominated headlines" (Platten, 2017:2).

Decisions to leave were not being taken lightly – and despite the assertions of many pro-remainers – were not motivated by racism and/or xenophobia, but by objective analyses of the various ways in which the EU has become an undemocratic and corrupt institution. For example, the Conservative MP, Sir William Cash (the main force behind the Maastricht Rebellion and in forcing the government to hold a referendum) used not to think that we should leave the EU, but changed his mind for a number of reasons – possibly the most important of which was a growing realisation that there was little or no appetite in Brussels to reform the EU, so the only alternative was to leave. As he explained in an interview in March 2015:

"There is 60% distrust in several countries. The turnout in the last EU elections was only 43% and that was including older people and compulsory voting. The number of people 20-35 years old who turned out voluntarily demonstrates a complete rejection of the system. People are rejecting it, and the ideologues in the establishment are refusing to listen. European Parliament decisions are not based on national voters decisions...I see the whole thing as a sort of constitutional fraud" (Briggs, 2015).

On the other side of the political fence, there were also strong and reasoned arguments to leave; according to Lord David Owen, Brexit was necessary as the risks of remaining in the EU were infinitely greater than the risks of leaving (Pearson, 2016a:27) – and Owen is uniquely placed to comment, having been both Minister for Europe and later Foreign Secretary in the Labour government of James Callaghan.

This book will show how the EU has gradually assumed greater powers and influence in the domestic and international affairs of member states, and how this influence has been achieved incrementally, bringing in changes over the last sixty years that have all led towards the development of a Federal European 'superstate' – The United States of Europe. The electorate has been deliberately kept in the dark with regard to this ultimate objective, as to have announced it would have likely led to intense opposition from member states, and possibly deterred those who were considering applying for membership.

The people who run the EU (as opposed to the Members of the European Parliament – MEPs), think that they have an important role to play in the social restructuring of Europe; whether they are correct or not is debatable – the point is that the peoples of Europe have not been consulted. This arrogant and morally corrupt (if not illegal) policy has no place in democratic societies in the 21st century; one cannot help but suspect that if a similar approach were adopted by an African or Latin American regime, the EU (probably through one of its many highly-paid Ambassadors), would be amongst the first to lecture those countries as to the necessity of democratic consultation with the electorate.

There has been no consultation, so we can only speculate as to the reasons for this abrogation of democratic accountability: perhaps because those concerned feel they know what is best for us – highly likely in view of the generally 'patronising' and arrogant attitude emanating from Brussels. More cynical observers might even question whether those involved in making these decisions (politicians, EU functionaries, CEOs of multinational organisations) gain some personal benefit from continued integration?

It is ironic that, whilst the original signatories of the 1957 Treaty felt they were shaping a 'brave new world' that would lead to peace and prosperity in Europe, the reality is that the EU increasingly appears to have lost its way, and has become an overbearing, bullying, largely unaccountable and corrupt monolith, seeking ever-greater control in the affairs of member states, seemingly for the greater good of an elite who control the EU for their own personal prestige and financial benefit.

For many years, we were told that the EU is good for all member states – indeed we have been told so by every UK Prime Minister from Edward Heath to David Cameron – as it allows free trade, free movement of people, and the enhanced power and prestige that stems from being part of a wealthy and influential 'bloc' of countries.

The EU, we are assured, provides heightened job safety through legislation such as the 'European Working Time Directive' (EWTD), it safeguards our farmers through the 'Common Agricultural Policy' (CAP), our fish stocks through the 'Common Fisheries Policy' (CFP), and it has held sole responsibility for the negotiation of our international trade (exports and imports) through the Brussels – directed EU Trade Policy, which has been under the control of the EU

Commission since 1957 (*The Economist*, 2016g:38). The EU has a Commission or similar for every aspect of life, including atomic energy, currency, defence, diplomacy, education, employment, environmental protection, foreign aid, international policing, monetary policy, consumer protection legislation, justice, and space exploration – all are dealt with as part of a unified policy decided in Brussels, and which, we are assured, function for the greater wealth and well-being of Europe as a whole. This being the case, then one might be forgiven for assuming that the percentage of people voting to remain in 2016 would have increased, rather than decreased when compared with 1975.

When the UK joined the European Economic Community (EEC) – also referred to as 'The Common Market' – in January 1973, Prime Minister Edward Heath claimed that it would enable the country to "... be more efficient and more competitive in gaining more markets not only in Europe but in the rest of the world" (BBC, 1973). Despite appearances to the contrary, there was resistance to UK membership of the EEC, and platitudes such as those offered by Heath masked the extent of political unease related to issues of trade, protectionism, job losses, and the loss of sovereignty, and the 'European Question' dogged the remainder of Heath's government until the Conservative defeat a year later in 1974.

The new Labour Prime Minister Harold Wilson staked his position on continued membership of the EEC through a referendum a year after his election – hoping to settle the matter once and for all. In what was a decisive result, just over 67% of voters backed 'remain' (BBC, 1975); with such a clear level of support, it is puzzling why this should have been reversed (with, admittedly, a closer margin) some forty years later in June 2016, when the number voting to leave was 51.9% (17, 410, 742 votes), as against the 48.1% (16, 141, 241) who voted to remain[4] (BBC, 2016e).

Given the outcome of the referendum, it can only be concluded that something happened between 1975 and 2016 to sour the UK's relationship with the EU. This book discusses the problems with the EU, examines reasons why this relationship went wrong, and explains a result that was generally not predicted by most political commentators. Ironically, one leading EU politician, prior to the UK referendum, had identified a key consideration that was to swing the vote in favour of leave.

Donald Tusk, President of the European Council, admitted that the EU had been too 'obsessed' with 'instant and total integration' and that it had "...failed to notice that ordinary people, the citizens of Europe, do not share our Euro-enthusiasm..." (Pearson, 2016b:16). However, he was very much in the minority: following the results of the UK referendum, there was chaos in Brussels. As an Editorial in *The Daily Telegraph* noted, the leaders of the EU

4. The turnout for the referendum was 72.2%, and the number of spoiled ballot papers was 26,003.

were 'in denial' about what had happened, and could not see a connection between Brexit and the EU's attempt to impose political union on Europe. As the paper commented, one of the key problems is Juncker himself, who has too much power, and attempts to 'railroad' through legislation. It concluded that: "The Commission, which began as an administrative civil service, has been given far too much power to instigate policy and decide the direction of travel. It needs to be reined in and authority returned to where it should reside – with elected politicians" (Editorial, 2016e:19).

This is the real lesson of Brexit.

Brexit: KBO

CHAPTER 1 | THE BACKGROUND TO BREXIT

1.1. The Referendum

On the 23rd June, 2016 the UK voted to leave the EU – and nine months later, on 29th March 2017, Prime Minister Theresa May triggered article 50 of the Lisbon Treaty. Briefly, Article 50 states that:

"A Member State which decides to withdraw shall notify the European Council of its intention. In the light of the guidelines provided by the European Council, the Union shall negotiate and conclude an agreement with that State, setting out the arrangements for its withdrawal, taking account of the framework for its future relationship with the Union. That agreement shall be negotiated in accordance with Article 218 (3) of the Treaty on the Functioning of the European Union. It shall be concluded on behalf of the Union by the Council, acting by a qualified majority, after obtaining the consent of the European Parliament. The Treaties shall cease to apply to the State in question from the date of entry into force of the withdrawal agreement or, failing that, two years after the notification referred to in paragraph 2, unless the European Council, in agreement with the Member State concerned, unanimously decides to extend this period."[1]

In her letter to Donald Tusk[2], May said that the result of the referendum had "... received Royal Assent from Her Majesty The Queen..." and had been passed by Parliament on 13th March...". She wrote:

"Today, therefore...I hereby notify the European Council in accordance with Article 50(2) of the Treaty on European Union of the United Kingdom's intention to withdraw from the European Union. In addition, in accordance with the same Article 50(2) as applied by Article 106a of the Treaty Establishing the European Atomic Energy Community, I hereby notify the European Council of the United Kingdom's intention to withdraw from the European Atomic Energy Community."[3]

---

1. http://www.lisbon-treaty.org/wcm/the-lisbon-treaty/treaty-on-European-union-and-comments/title-6-final-provisions/137-article-50.html
2. Elected by European Heads of State, and approved by European Parliament; *not* elected by popular vote from amongst the citizens of the EU member states.
3. https://www.gov.uk/government/uploads/system/uploads/attachment_data/file/604079/Prime_Ministers_letter_to_European_Council_President_Donald_Tusk.pdf

This fired the 'starting gun' for a period of two years within which the terms and conditions of the UK's new relationship with the EU had to be completed. This meant that the UK Government had until 29th March 2019 to negotiate as much access to the European Single Market/Customs Union and to other EU organisations as it wishes and member states will permit.

However, both parties concerned (basically the EU and the UK) are only likely to arrive at a mutually-beneficial agreement if they have something to gain; the problem is that the EU does not wish the UK to leave, and will do everything in its power to make so-called 'negotiations' difficult (if not impossible), and subject to protraction in the hope that the political situation in the UK will be such that the current government falls. Ideally for Brussels, a new UK government would be more favourable to the EU project, and would nullify the results of the referendum – and possibly hold another referendum in the hope that the result would swing in favour of 'remain.' In this respect, the Labour party under Jeremy Corbyn is already talking about "... keeping the UK in the EU single market and customs union, perhaps indefinitely" (Grew and Pancevski, 2017).

If no agreement over trade can be reached then UK-EU trade will be conducted under the regulations set down by the World Trade Organisation (WTO)[4]. Indeed, Liam Fox (Secretary of State for International Trade) has already begun talks with the WTO, and with the USA (Wheeler, 2017:12): currently, the UK operates within the WTO framework as a member of the EU, and Fox is quoted as promising that the UK 'would seek to replicate as far as possible its current obligations to the WTO' (Blitz and Donnan, 2016:2), but at the same time, allowing it to develop future trading relations with non-EU countries.

This is generally portrayed by 'remainers' as a negative alternative, yet excluding EU member states, in 2016 there were 134 countries that were members of the WTO; in addition, there are another 25 (non-EU) countries that are currently negotiating membership terms (WTO, 2018). Thus, in the event of difficulties ensuring tariff-free trade with the EU, there are 134 non-EU countries that could become the focus of UK trading arrangements – and of greatest importance, this includes the world's two most economically powerful nations – the USA and China, in addition to key markets in all continents: Argentina, Brazil, Canada, Chile, Colombia and Mexico (in the Americas), Nigeria and South Africa (Africa), India, Japan, Singapore, South Korea and Taiwan (Asia), Bahrain, Jordan, Kuwait, Oman, Saudi Arabia, and the UAE (Middle East), and Australia and New Zealand in the Pacific.

Furthermore, it might be good for the UK to focus outside Europe – regions such as Latin America and Asia have huge, rapidly-growing populations, which will provide excellent markets for UK products.

---

4. https://www.wto.org/english/thewto_e/whatis_e/tif_e/fact2_e.htm

1.2. Why did the UK Vote to Leave?

Whilst the previous section dealt with the facts underlying the referendum, what is perhaps of greater interest, is *why* the UK voted to leave, despite all predictions and exhortations to the contrary. In the final analysis, it would appear that there were many reasons, and doubtless there will be intensive discussion of this decision over the coming years.

Judging by articles in the press (a barometer of public opinion) in the lead up to the referendum, the major reasons for public dissatisfaction remained those that had existed previously, but were now supplemented by others based on experiences of life under EU 'diktat':

Fears of unrestricted immigration
(Ganesh, 2014; Dominiczak, 2014b; Cavendish, 2015; Moore, 2015; Mulholland and Webb, 2015; BBC, 2016b; Bulman and Fenton, 2016; Dominiczak and Holehouse, 2016; Editorial, 2016a; Hope and Barrett, 2016; Johnston, 2016b; Kelley, 2016; Mason, 2016a; McDonald, 2016; Swinford, 2016a; Economist, 2016a; Politi, 2017) **and the threat this poses to British culture and society** (Dominiczak, 2015; Editorial, 2016a; Palmer, 2012; Hope, 2014).

Corruption/lack of accountability/transparency on the part of the Brussels machinery (Charlemagne, 2010; and Jowit, 2012; BBC, 2014; Pop, 2014; Holehouse, 2015d and 2016b; Cash, 2016; Editorial, 2016c; Hughes, 2016a; **Rankin, 2016a;** Birnbaum, 2016).

The EU wants total political integration: the 'United States of Europe' (Lamont, 1994; Booker and North, 2003; McNamara, 2010; Booker , 2015; Cash, 2016; Zalan, 2016; Chazan, 2016; Glapinski, 2017)

Excessive (and unnecessary) bureaucracy/regulations (Clarke, 2014; Waterfield, 2014b; Editorial, 2016b and 2016d; Pickard and Hollinger, 2016; Birnbaum, 2016; and Crisp, 2017; Rayner and Hope, 2017)

EU "interference" in UK laws (BBC, 2012a; Dominiczak and Waterfield, 2014; Howard and Aikens, 2016; Swinford, 2016d; Barker *et. al*, 2017; and Crisp, 2017).

The Common Agricultural and Fisheries policies (Gorton et. al., 2000): **give unfair advantage to many EU farmers, and allows EU fishing fleets to**

'plunder' UK waters (Ungoed-Thomas and Leake, 2013; BSF, 2016; Boffey, 2017a; McLean, 2017; *The Economist*, 2017b).

Excessive financial demands on member states – much of which is ultimately wasted (Charlemagne, 2010; Birnbaum, 2016; Bennett *et. al.*, 2017; Editorial, 2017a)

The loss of control over external trade deals (Lilley, 2016; *The Economist*, 2017g; Wheeler, 2017)

EU ignores the views of the electorate (Birnbaum, 2016; Editorial, 2016b)

These were key motivators to vote 'leave'; the 'remainers' have argued (and will doubtless continue to argue) that many of these accusations are untrue or exaggerated, and as such, should never have been taken seriously by the electorate. If this is indeed the case, one has to ask why, given the number of intelligent and articulate 'remainers', they did not succeed in persuading voters that these issues were manufactured by the popular press, rather than being a true reflection of the actual situation?

During the 2016 referendum campaign, many people complained that the public were not presented with the information they needed on which to base an intelligent and informed decision; this is a valid criticism, and one that continues to be levelled at both 'leave' and 'remain' camps. The problem was that nobody could say with any degree of certainty exactly what would happen were we to leave the EU.

It was impossible to predict the politico-economic consequences of such a complex decision (and one that had never been made before), as multiple factors (many of which were not apparent at the time) have a considerable effect on the outcome. Nor can we even be sure that life would revert to how it had been prior to joining the EU, as the world has changed so much since 1973.

1.3. The Future Direction of the EU?

1.3.1. Introduction

As a basis for their argument to remain in the EU, many sought to assure EU sceptics that the current relationship would not be subject to further (deeper and/or wider) integration in the future. This assertion could be neither proven nor disproven; however, judging by the constant changes over the last thirty years (in terms of both membership of the EU and of Brussels' legislation), it is very unlikely that things would stand still over the *next* 10-30 years. In January 2016

David Cameron tried to negotiate on four main areas – identified as causing considerable concern amongst voters:

1. An 'emergency brake' on in-work benefits for EU citizens who were working in the UK.

2. A halt to the payment of child benefits to people working in the UK, but whose children were living elsewhere.

3. Safeguards to ensure that those countries outside the Eurozone were not subject to the increasing financial regulations associated with the Euro.

4. That the UK would not be forced into ever-closer union, in line with the EU federalist objectives.

Overall, he failed in two objectives, had a partial victory in one, and a greater victory in another. The emergency brake – which had become a political 'hot potato' – was agreed, but only for no more than seven years, without the possibility of extension, and as such, could not really be counted as a victory.

Child benefits would not be stopped, but instead would be index-linked to the cost of living of the country in which they were based – overall this would probably have meant a small *decrease* in payments, but the principle of payments remained unaltered.

He partially won on the exclusion of non-Eurozone countries from Euro legislation, and seemed to have won completely on halting further EU integration. Naturally, on returning to the UK, Cameron presented this as a victory, and doubtless hoped that it would take the wind out of the pro-referendum lobby's sails. However, his 'victory' was not seen in quite the same light throughout the country, nor even by members of his own Party.

As Parker and Barker (2016) observed, whilst Downing Street can "… justifiably claim that the Prime Minister has achieved many of his original negotiating goals…" according to Eurosceptics, this "…is only because the things he wanted were so trivial in the first place."

Furthermore, as Tylecote and Cash (2016:235) point out, any concessions that he may have won were worthless in any case, as explained in a briefing paper published on 8th March by the House of Commons Library, in which it was noted that the deal:

"Does not bind the EU institutions, and is not necessarily legally enforceable under either EU or domestic law. It could be very problematic if either the Court of Justice of the EU or a domestic court found an inconsistency between the Decision and the EU Treaties. The Decision...cannot guarantee all of the outcomes envisaged in it."

Cameron was unsuccessful, largely due to the intransigence on the part of the EU hierarchy, which undoubtedly contributed to a 'leave' vote in the referendum later that year, and to Brexit. Indeed, Cameron himself is reported as having said that one of the key reasons why so many people voted 'leave' was that " ... there was no control over freedom of movement" (Dominiczak and Holehouse, 2016: 1). *The Daily Telegraph* (Editorial, 2016b: 23) pulled no punches: "The EU leadership has decided that the future lies with greater integration, so even the smallest reform will be regarded as a challenge to this philosophy. Ironically, the negotiations with Britain have only highlighted how absurd this dream of a totally united Europe looks."

1.3.2. Further Integration

Whilst it is impossible to be certain what will happen in the future, judging by past performance and current pronouncements about the future, it is likely that there *will* be a mixture of both deeper and wider integration – probably with the candidate states from the Balkans joining simultaneously – and moves to force all states that have not already done so, to adopt the Euro by 2025. There are two probable directions of future travel:

Deeper integration: towards a United States of Europe, underpinned by a common currency – in this sense, the adoption of the Euro was one of many steps along the road to integration for, as McNamara (2010) observes: "No monetary union has ever succeeded without concurrent political union – including fiscal consolidation." In 2016, an article in the *EUobserver* appeared to conform that that deeper integration was needed (Zalan, 2016).

Wider integration: this would extend the EU to include European nations that are not yet members – most probably those nations that are currently 'in the queue' to join: Albania, Kosovo, Montenegro, Serbia, and Turkey. However since the recent coup attempt in Turkey and the assumption of dictatorial powers by President Erdoğan (Filkins, 2017), even the EU will have to put Turkey's membership 'on hold' for the foreseeable future.

Evidence for further integration is not difficult to find: for example, Jean-Claude Juncker was instrumental in the publication of a 'White Paper' in which a variety of proposals were examined for closer European integration following the exit of the UK. However, despite what Juncker may think, a post-Brexit scenario will be unlikely to make his life any easier. Cleppe (2017), writing in the Belgian paper *Le Soir* pointed out some uncomfortable truths for the EU Commission, relating to the current levels of dissatisfaction with EU membership amongst member states. He suggested that it was not just the UK that opposed further integration/ expansion, but also the "... anti-establishment parties across Europe..." He said that in "...Italy or Austria, such parties may be even closer to power. Needless to say, Juncker hasn't listed the option of turning the EU... into a mere trade – facilitating arrangement – a vision that may have kept the British in if it had ever been presented. According to a Pew poll, a majority in EU countries want to return powers from the EU back to member states."

Juncker is an avowed Federalist, whose vision is one state called Europe, with a number of politically (and economically) subservient 'regions'. This is understandable, as Juncker is a former Prime Minister of Luxembourg – a landlocked country, surrounded by Belgium, France, and Germany, with basically a mixture of French and German cultures, reflected in the fact that it has three official languages: Luxembourgish, French, and German. Luxembourg was incapable of defending itself in World War 2 when it was invaded and occupied by the Germans for four years. Given this historical heritage, it is no wonder that Juncker feels more at home as part of a larger Franco-German alliance, in which his country can have an influence far in excess of its actual social, political, economic, military and cultural weight.

Despite the potential dangers that Brexit represents to the continued stability of the EU, rather than pushing for greater autonomy and national decision-making in his 'State of the Union' address to the EU Parliament in Strasbourg in September 2017, Juncker called on all EU states to join the Euro, and for the creation of a European Finance Minister, in addition to a widening of the Schengen passport-free travel area. He also suggested that, by 2025 the EU would have "... a fully-fledged European defence union..." which he claimed was needed, and that NATO wanted it (Boffey, 2017b). It is highly unlikely that this is true, and furthermore, in view of the befuddled and confused EU policy towards external threats, it is undoubtedly safer to leave the defence of the West in NATO, rather than EU hands – yet Juncker continues to present speculation as facts, a clear case of what Winston Churchill labelled 'terminological inexactitude.'

One of the most potentially dangerous suggestions Juncker made was to combine "...the presidencies of the European commission and the European council ..." claiming that "...the EU needed to be more flexible and streamlined..." and that "Europe would be easier to understand if one captain was steering the ship" (Boffey, 2017b). Whilst one might assume that modesty forbade him from suggesting who this 'captain' might be, such a suggestion could hardly be described as 'slowing' the process of European integration! Nigel Farage MEP, the former UKIP leader, found Junker's speech 'worrying'. As he explained: "More

Europe in every single direction and all of it to be done without the consent of the people.... All I can say, is thank God we are leaving. You have learned nothing from Brexit. If you had given ...Cameron concessions, particularly on immigration, the Brexit vote, I must admit, would never, never have happened" (Boffey, 2017b).

It could, therefore, be suggested that the intransigence of the EU is directly responsible for the departure of the UK, and it is highly unlikely that EU integration will remain in its current state. There are, however, some EU politicians who oppose deeper integration: in early 2016, the German Finance Minister Wolfgang Schäuble cautioned against deeper integration should the UK vote to leave: he suggested that a vote for Brexit should be seen "...as a warning and a wake-up call not to go on with business as usual."

In what was an apparent reference to the intransigence of Juncker, Schäuble said that there would be no popular support for deeper EU integration following a Brexit vote "...except maybe in Luxembourg" (Chazan, 2016:8).

Chapter 2 | "Project Fear"

2.1. Introduction

Those who wanted to remain in the EU did all that they could to dissuade voters from opting for Brexit. There is nothing wrong with putting forward ones' point of view, preferably backed up by verifiable facts and statistics – a healthy debate was what was required; this was not, however, what we got. Instead, we were treated to shameless displays of so-called facts, used to present the case to leave or go: both sides presented distorted 'facts', but in the case of those who wished to remain, the campaign plumbed new depths of misinformation, scare tactics, and in some cases, downright lies. It would appear that those trying to scare the population into voting to remain, did so as it was in their interests to remain, and not necessarily the interests of the nation as a whole.

Charles Moore, writing in *The Daily Telegraph* felt that many 'remainers' did not understand Brexit, and that many of what he referred to as the 'bigoted elite' had not even considered whether there was case for leaving the EU (Moore, 2016:16), so certain were they that only "swivel-eyed loons"[1] would be stupid enough to even consider leaving.

There was obviously intense discussion of Brexit in the UK Press – the political affiliations of which are widely understood, and generally accepted; broadly speaking, the more right-wing publications (such as *The Daily Telegraph*) tended to favour 'leave', whilst those of the left-wing (*The Guardian*), favoured 'remain'.[2] Whichever side they came down on, their final recommendation was generally (in their view) the best option for the country as a whole. There was a third strand of persuasion however, which was the serious business press – such as the *Financial Times* and *The Economist*; interestingly both tended to favour 'remain', possibly as their decision was influenced by big business concerns, rather than a recognition of the fears and concerns of ordinary people.

Whilst such a viewpoint was understandable, it was less than honest to claim that their conclusions were based on objective analyses, and that their recommendations would be beneficial to the country as a whole. For example, *The Economist* backed 'remain', possibly reflecting the vested interests of much of its readership. In a referendum special, designed to swing its readership behind the 'remainers', the journal claimed to "...believe in the importance of objective analysis and reasoned argument..." but appeared to undermine this claim by

---

1. "Swivel-eyed loons" was apparently a derogatory slur made against members of UKIP in May 2013, by an unnamed senior Conservative politician – the person concerned was (unwisely) publicly defended by David Cameron, who himself became associated with the remark.
2. Papers backing 'leave' included: *The Daily Telegraph, The Sunday Telegraph, The Times, The Sunday Times, The Daily Mail, The Mail on Sunday*, and *The Sun*; 'remain backers included: *The Guardian, Financial Times, The Observer, The Mail on Sunday, The Daily Mirror* (Ridley, 2016).

admitting in the same paragraph that it was "...not neutral: we are convinced that a decision to leave (a so-called Brexit) would be bad for Britain, Europe and the world" (*The Economist*, 2016b). It then proceeded to present a series of what it described as 'summaries' of the evidence. A close reading of these summaries suggests that some were speculative statements – for example, it was suggested (under the heading 'Euroscepticism') that "Hostility to the EU in Britain is different from anything found on the continent."

As will be made clear later, this is debatable as there are many people in continental member states who are vehemently opposed to the EU – in the last French Presidential elections, Marine Le Pen secured around 33% of the national vote – running on an anti-EU ticket. Furthermore, even if one were to take the claim at face value, it must surely serve to underline the fact that the UK is different to Continental Europe, and as such, membership of the EU – which involves a loss of sovereignty – is undesirable?

With regard to trade, it was claimed that a "...Post-Brexit Britain would probably end up with fewer and worse trade deals than it has now..." – this was sheer speculation, as at the time there was no evidence to support this assertion. The journal also claimed that, even if the UK left the EU, it would not be able to prevent EU immigration into the UK – a provocative statement targeted at the major fear of many who voted to leave. This is illogical, as when the UK leaves, it will no longer have control of its borders dictated by Brussels, and will be able to control immigration through the mechanisms of tourist, employment and residency visas, and long- and short-term work permits – the same way in which most countries of the world control immigration.

The lack of facts led to uncertainty amongst the UK public, who were consequently forced to rely on the only 'facts' they knew – their perceptions and experiences of the ways in which membership of the EU had influenced their lives. For the majority of the British, the EU is an unelected 'busybody', constantly interfering in people's lives, and inventing unnecessary regulations simply to justify their own salaries. Witness the controversy over 'bendy' bananas and later 'bendy' cucumbers. In effect, EU legislation did not ban these, but insisted that they were sold according to quality grading regulations – which take shape into account[3]. Many things emerge from this: one that the EU has communicated the legislation so badly that elements of the UK press and population have

---

3. Commission Regulation 2257/94 identifies certain restrictions for fruits that producers have to conform to in order to sell their produce within the EU. The regulation states that bananas must be "free from malformation or abnormal curvature." Class 1 bananas can have "slight defects of shape" and Class 2 bananas full-on "defects of shape". In 2011 this regulation and other relevant rules were brought together for the sake of clarity under a single implementing regulation (1333/2011), and in 2013 a further change simplified reporting requirements (implementing regulation 565/2013). Source: The European Parliament Information Office in London (26th May, 2016); see: http://www.Europarl.Europa.eu/unitedkingdom/en/media/Euromyths/bendybananas.html

misunderstood; secondly, it reflects the overall negative perception of the EU – that the UK public is willing to largely believe anything regardless of how stupid it may sound, connected with Brussels.

Attitudes such as this willingness to believe that Brussels is capable of producing such legislation take time to form, and are based on some elements of truth: either way, the EU is ultimately responsible – for poor communication of the facts, and for having a track record of devising unnecessary and unwanted legislation. People tend to automatically perceive this as being simply another example of EU interference. Finally, why was the legislation necessary in the first place? International traders have managed for hundreds (if not thousands) of years without the interference of the Brussels bureaucrats – all they appear to be doing is to justify their salaries and expense accounts by devising unwarranted and unwanted legislation.

Having said this, there are real examples of where EU legislation is slowly eroding elements of British culture that have been with us for centuries – such as the imposition of metric weights and measures in 1985: this stemmed from the EU Directive 80/181/EEC[4], which gave the UK until 1994 to introduce metric measurements. Another EU directive gave the UK until March 2015 to ensure that all road width and height restriction warning signs were presented in meters and centimetres as well as in feet and inches – as it will cost councils more to make both imperial and metric warning signs, and as EU law takes precedent over national law, it is likely that imperial measurements will be gradually phased out on UK roads. Whilst distances in the UK are currently measured in miles, one can envisage a situation in the near future in which Brussels legislates that roadside distance signposts (ie. distances to cities/towns) must be given in kilometres rather than in miles.

With regard to liquid measurements, the absurd situation exists in which we buy petrol in litres, yet vehicles sold in the UK give consumption figures in miles per gallon. In addition to these anomalies, companies such as McDonald's are still allowed to sell quarter pounder burgers. Furthermore, we can still buy a pint of beer in a pub, as no government has yet sought to change this – to do so would almost certainly result in defeat at the following general election, as the term 'a pint' is so deeply ingrained in British culture. An example of Brussels' most recent interference is the legislation designed to prevent the sale of vacuum cleaners that consume more than 900 watts of power (Morley and Crisp, 2017: 1): this led to a run on sales of the more powerful machines before the cut-off date of 1st September 2017. Overall, it is probably fair to say that the UK public's general perception of the EU is at best neutral, and at worst highly negative – few people view the EU in an overall positive light and their negative experiences

4. "Council Directive 80/181/EEC: On the Approximation of the Laws of the Member States Relating to Units of Measurement and on the Repeal of Directive 71/354/EEC" . The Council of the European Communities. 20 December 1979.

of the EU far outweigh the positive. In a highly-perceptive piece in *The Sunday Times*, Dominic Lawson identified the differences in perceptions that 'leavers' had of the EU when compared with 'remainers.' The former group had been outrageously pilloried in the Press (and especially in remain-supporting media such as the BBC).

Lawson commented that, in February 2017 a BBC correspondent revealed that "... a statistical analysis of the data obtained for over a thousand individual local government wards confirms how the strength of the 'leave' vote was strongly associated with lower educational qualifications..." (Lawson, 2017:20): the implication being that the majority of 'leavers' were not as well-educated as 'remainers', and *ipso facto* could not really be expected to understand what they were voting for and why.

One might make similar observations linking education levels and voting patterns in UK General Elections, yet this has not been done – why not? If commentators were to proceed down such dangerous paths, they would run the risk of offending certain groups within the population, and, perhaps more seriously, risk undermining the very democracy on which the stability of UK society rests – that the public, through universal suffrage (as opposed to educational qualifications) – elects the government. As Lawson pointed out, it is highly unlikely that the 'better educated' remainers knew then (or indeed now) more about the institution of which they voted to remain a member – he asked, rhetorically:

"How many of these more educated men and women had thought deeply about the nature of the institutions of the EU, studied the texts of the Maastricht and Lisbon treaties, explored the composition of the European Court of Justice and read up on how the *acquis communautare*[5] works? How many could name the five Presidents of the EU, and define what exactly each of them actually does? I am sure the answer is very few. Instead their thinking will have been as conditioned by group-think and sentiment as any of their less educated compatriots who voted for Brexit" (Lawson, 2017:20).

---

5. *Acquis communautaire* is a French term referring to the cumulative body of European Community laws, comprising the EC's objectives, substantive rules, policies and, in particular, the primary and secondary legislation and case law – all of which form part of the legal order of the European Union (EU). This includes all the treaties, regulations and directives passed by the European institutions, as well as judgements laid down by the European Court of Justice. The acquis is dynamic, constantly developing as the Community evolves, and fundamental. All Member States are bound to comply with the *acquis communautaire*" (https://www.Eurofound.Europa.eu/observatories/eurwork/industrial-relations-dictionary/acquis-communautaire).

2.2. The Economy

2.2.1. Employment, Housing, Mortgages, Pensions and Taxation

There were so many doom-laden scenarios and threats made by those who wished us to remain in the EU, that it is not really possible to detail them all here. A few of the more high-profile threats, however, related to the economy and employment: David Cameron, for instance, based his strategy on instilling an element of uncertainty if not fear in the population, by suggesting dire economic consequences if they voted 'leave' (Swinford, and Holehouse, 2015:12).

He issued a blanket warning in May 2016 that a vote for Brexit could see UK households being £4,300 worse off (Riley-Smith, 2016:9). Other threats included those by George Osborne (the then-Chancellor of the Exchequer) who claimed that, in the event of a 'leave vote', house prices would fall by between 10 and 18%, whilst the ratings agency Fitch forecast a 25% fall, and Mark Carney, the Governor of the Bank of England claimed that mortgage costs would rise (Fraser, 2016); despite being an avid 'remainer', and a key member of the 'Project fear' cabal, Carney changed sides not long after the result, stating, in September 2016, that he could see 'large' trade opportunities for the UK following Brexit (Wallace, 2016b:37).

He was obviously being less than truthful before or after the referendum, as the two opinions are totally contradictory: either way, it does not exactly inspire confidence to hear of such indecision (or apparent mendacity) from the man who is in charge of the nation's banks.

George Osborne also claimed that mortgages would rise (Chan, 2016a:31), and in addition threatened to introduce an emergency budget and increase taxation; four days after the vote, on 27th June, he publicly admitted that he had no plans to do this (Nelson, 2016). He also upset pensioners, claiming that if we voted to leave, they would lose up £32,000 worth of their pensions (Swinford, 2016f:11) – a rather nasty threat to a vulnerable group, and one based on speculation. At a more strategic level, Osborne was reported to have been "... pushing the Group of 20 leading economies to warn about the dangers of the UK leaving the EU..." (Giles and Waldmeir, 2016: 1). Commentators such as Wallace pointed out that, two months after the referendum result, and despite the apocalyptic predictions that would follow a Brexit vote: "It all looks like business as usual so far" (2016a:29). As an editorial in the *Financial Times* (largely a 'remain' supporter) was forced to admit: "...the Remain campaign and a host of independent forecasters warned that a Leave vote would inflict immediate pain to the [UK] economy. In the event, aided by a prompt loosening of monetary policy by the Bank of England, the UK rode the shock without too much difficulty..." (Editorial, 2017c: 10).

Another 'scare' attempt was the assertion by the Chairman of the European

Securities and Markets Authority that a post-Brexit UK would find it difficult to sell funds across Europe (Flood, 2016). In March 2016, Black Rock forecast that the 'economy would be hit hard by a vote to leave the EU, with equities, sterling and the London property market all likely to suffer' (Parker and Allen, 2016:4).

In a similar vein, according to Duke and Smith (2017: 2), Credit Suisse "... warned of the dangers of a recession in Britain...". The day before the referendum, Janet Yellen, Chairman of the US Federal Reserve, appeared to suggest that a Brexit vote could lead to another world recession (Spence and Tovey, 2016:B1) – a threat designed to hit potential 'leavers' in their pockets, whist at the same time, instilling in them a sense of potential responsibility for the future. In February 2016, the Environment Secretary, Liz Truss, warned on the BBC's *Question Time* political debate programme that a vote for Brexit would be like entering the "Twilight Zone" (Lawson, 2016a: 20), and this sort of scaremongering has continued post-referendum.

Economic commentators such as David Smith (*The Sunday Times*) seemed to sum up all the economic arguments for remaining in the EU, dismissing many 'leave' arguments as 'myths', and he suggested that the 'Leave' movement "...has been outnumbered, out-analysed, out-argued and technically out-classed by the Treasury, OECD, IMF, LSE, PwC, IFS and others. The evidence suggests, convincingly, that there will be both a short-term economic shock and long-term economic damage from leaving the EU" (Smith, 2016:4). What he failed to acknowledge, however, was that the organisations he listed have vested interests in the UK remaining within the EU, so perhaps their predictions might have been motivated by something other than concerns over the future of a post-Brexit UK? The BBC (2016d), to its credit, noted that the constant 'drip-feed' of threats actually had a counter-productive effect, as many people did not believe them and resented being threatened.

2.2.2. The IMF

Whilst it is understandable that UK companies that operate internationally might not welcome Brexit, there was far less justification for the interference of a number of non-UK organisations 'warning' UK voters of the danger to the UK economy should we vote to leave. One such organisation was the high-profile International Monetary Fund (IMF), which in December 2015 warned against a 'leave' vote: Christine Lagarde, Head of the IMF said that she very much hoped the UK would stay in the EU, and suggested that the UK's economic progress could be badly affected by Brexit (Spence, 2015:37).

This same message was repeated in April 2016, and she suggested that leaving the EU could lead to disrupted trading relationships, and a loss of confidence in the UK as an international investment centre (BBC, 2016a). Lagarde threatened to publish an IMF report warning of the risk of Brexit a week before the referendum vote – this was obviously designed to influence voters; the Eurosceptic Employment Minister Priti Patel took the IMF to task, pointing out that, "The EU-funded IMF should not interfere in our democratic debate a week before polling day. It appears the Chancellor is cashing in favours to Ms Lagarde in order to encourage the IMF to bully the British people" (Giles, 2016).

In addition Lagarde suggested that Brexit would lead to a 'steep fall in house prices' and a stock market crash (Swinford and Chan, 2016:8), and she reportedly said that a vote to leave could lead to "...sharp drops in equity and house prices, increased borrowing costs for households and businesses..." (Chan, 2016b:39). The greatest fall in house prices would be likely to be within the Greater London district (largely 'remain' territory) – so would hardly concern voters in the Midlands and north-east (strong 'Brexit' areas), and for those that were finding it difficult to afford a house within Greater London, a fall in prices might actually be welcome.

The IMF predictions were welcomed by George Osborne, who claimed that the organisation "... has given us the clearest independent warning of the taste of bad things to come if we leave the EU..." and by David Cameron, who claimed that the "... IMF is right – leaving the EU would pose major risks for the UK economy" (Ahmed, 2016). This is the same IMF that, in 2013 issued warnings over the Cameron-Osborne approach to the UK's deficit, suggesting that the austerity policy would lead to a double-dip recession (Burke, 2013). On this occasion, the IMF was slammed by Osborne, who contradicted their assessment (Mason, 2013); the IMF was proven wrong, forcing Lagarde to publicly admit the error the following year (Armitstead, 2014).

The next year the IMF returned to their criticism of Osborne's austerity policies in 2015 (Giugliano, 2015), and were once again proven wrong, as the UK then had one of the lowest rates of unemployment in Europe, and one of the best-performing economies. A former Chancellor of the Exchequer, Lord Lamont dismissed the IMF's concerns as "...assertions...for which there is no real evidence"; he added that the IMF was "...very closely connected to the European Union..." and was, therefore, bound to reflect the views of the EU. This point was also made by Nigel Farage, the then-leader of the United Kingdom Independence Party (UKIP), who put it more forcefully, declaring that the IMF had been "...effectively hijacked..." by pro-EU bosses. The IMF appeared to confirm its partiality one month after the referendum result, when it claimed that Brexit would "...exert a drag on Eurozone growth for three years..." (Chan, 2016c: 35), showing that its concern lay more with growth in the Eurozone, than with growth in the UK.

The IMF continues to attempt to undermine Brexit, over a year after the referendum result, with a 'warning' in early 2018 that the UK must make "...

sweeping reforms to pensions, the planning system, infrastructure, education, training, and research and development if it wants to boost economic growth in the years to come..." (Wallace, 2018:3). The message is basically that the whole country is in need of an overhaul – yet, as observed earlier, the UK is doing at least as well as our European neighbours, if not better in some areas.

In March 2018, Lagarde – possibly mindful of the effects on the Eurozone economy of Brexit – suggested a 'rainy day' fund, which she compared to car insurance: members would contribute up to 0.35 % of their GDP on an annual basis, which would then be saved (it was not clear who would hold this money) to be used to 'cushion' member states against the effects of a future economic downturn. Needless to say, the idea went down badly in what the *Financial Times* described as a coalition of "... eight fiscally conservative member states led by the Netherlands...." which complained that they would end up paying for the 'profligacy' for other, less financially-conscientious member states (Jones and Khan, 2018:7).

Taking at face value the comments on the IMF made by Lamont and Farage, this might explain the organisation's attitude as expressed publicly by Lagarde. The real economic problem, as far as the EU is concerned, is not that Brexit will damage the UK's economy, but that it will damage the economies of most of those countries that remain. This is the reason why the EU negotiators are currently trying to extract billions of pounds from the UK, as part of a so-called 'divorce bill.' In July 2017, a full year after the Brexit vote, the IMF went on a 'damage limitation' offensive, as it was then obvious that the UK would leave the EU, and equally obvious that the intransigence of the Eurocrats might well result in trade being conducted under WTO rules, rather than both sides agreeing to some form of 'Free Trade' deal.

As will become apparent in Chapter 6.3. ("Free Trade or Tariffs"), the UK trade deficit with the EU is something that in normal circumstances would be considered unwelcome for the UK; yet there had been no evidence of this worrying the IMF prior to Brexit. However, when the IMF suddenly announced that the UK should 'bring down its large current account deficit' (Wallace, 2017: 33) as to maintain it would be dangerous for Britain, it became obvious what was happening: Brussels was worried that following the UK withdrawal, and the continuation of trade on WTO terms, the EU would lose out considerably, as it sells far more to the UK than we sell to them (the 'trade' or 'current account' deficit).

This would be far worse for the EU than it would for the UK, so Brussels has called in favours from the IMF, and sent it out to do battle against the potentially damaging effects on the EU of WTO-based trading regulations: the EU has pressurised the IMF to get the UK to alter this trade imbalance before the end of the two – year exit period. In other words, when the EU and IMF speak about 'danger' or a 'very bad' economic future, they are more likely to be considering the danger to themselves.

Then there is the issue of the UK's contribution to EU funds. Following the two year negotiation period during which details of withdrawal are agreed, the UK's net contribution, estimated at £13-billion in 2016[6] will have to be paid by other countries after Brexit. Bennett *et. al.*, (2017), using figures from The Treasury, suggested a figure of £12.9-billion – broadly agreeing with the £13-billion mentioned earlier. In part, it is claimed that the figure owed by the UK to the EU is a direct consequence of the former UK PM Tony Blair, as, according to Dominiczak (2014a): "The UK's contributions to the European Union have doubled in the past five years in part due to Tony Blair's decision to cut Britain's rebate from Brussels.... Britain's net contribution last year [2013] was £8.6-billion, up from £4.3-billion in 2009."

This was a consequence of Blair's "... decision to agree to a 7 per cent cut in the rebate during negotiations on the last EU budget deal" (Dominiczak, 2014a). The obvious question to ask is why should a British Prime Minister (who should be putting the interests of his country above all others) give away part of a rebate that it took Margaret Thatcher tough negotiations to achieve? Perhaps the answer lies in the reported attempts by Blair to run for the position of EU President (Hope, 2012; Wintour, 2014) – on a previous occasion his candidacy was blocked by the Benelux countries (Waterfield, 2009b) – so one might speculate that this was his way of currying favour with the EU, at the expense of the British taxpayer, to enable him to make another bid at a later date. In addition, of course, for him to become EU President, the UK would still have to be an EU member, which also might account for Blair's attempts to overturn the result of the referendum (BBC, 2017a; Mason, 2017; Swinford, 2017a:4; Swinford and Watson, 2017).

2.2.3. Increases in Unemployment

In January 2014 increases in unemployment were forecast, with the CEO of Nestlé claiming that a withdrawal from the EU would be bad for UK industry, and implying that the company might have to re-consider its position in the UK (Kleinman, 2014); by August 2016, however, his successor was downplaying such warnings, claiming that when Nestlé goes into a country, it does so 'forever' (Chan, 2016d). In March 2016, BMW warned its employees that in the event of a 'leave' vote, thousands of workers at Rolls Royce factories might find their jobs threatened (Johnston, 2016a). Fast forward to 24th June, and BMW announced that there would be "...no immediate threat..." to UK worker's jobs (Boston, 2016).

In June 2016, J.P. Morgan's Jamie Dimon warned that in the event of a Brexit vote, 'large numbers' of staff would leave the UK – yet no evidence for this

---

6. https://fullfact.org/Europe/our-eu-membership-fee-55-million/)

assertion has subsequently emerged. As Allister Heath (Deputy Editor of *The Daily Telegraph*) pointed out:

"We were also told, repeatedly, that several large banks would quit London as a result of the post credit-crunch regulatory and tax backlash. HSBC spent a long time and a lot of money considering its HQ location, and there was talk that Standard Chartered and even Barclays might leave. Nothing happened – in fact, HSBC's high-profile decision to stay was the final nail in the coffin of that bank exodus idea" (Heath, 2016).

In a January 2016 survey of 700 British and German companies operating in the UK, 29% said they would "...either reduce capacities in the UK or relocate altogether in the event of a Brexit." Within the survey, it appeared that IT and technology sector companies were most likely to leave: "...41% say they would consider decreasing capacity or relocating..." (Oltermann, 2016); to date (April 2018), no such mass flight appears to have happened. Other high-profile companies that have promised to stay in the UK despite Brexit, include the Spanish telecommunications giant Telefónica (Fildes, 2017:20), in addition to the news in June 2017 that Rolls-Royce had decided not to build its new experimental test bed abroad, but in Derby, rejuvenating the site which should eventually provide some 12,000 jobs (Hollinger, 2017:18).

What is happening, however, is that by April 2018 there had been what *The Sunday Times* described as a "...significant shift in the location of the leading companies..." away from London, in particular to the Midlands and North (Tyler, 2018:I). Figures from the Office for National Statistics (ONS) show that in the three months since the referendum vote (June-September, 2016), the British economy grew by 0.05%, (BBC, 2016f), taxes did not rise, and on 2nd November 2017, the Bank of England doubled the UK interest rate to 0.5% – the first rate rise in ten years, and reflective of the healthy state of the economy.

Another major change was in exchange rates: Stirling fell in value against both the Euro and the US Dollar, making British goods cheaper abroad and therefore generally more attractive, but this is a 'double-edged' sword, as many exporters of manufactured goods have to import their raw materials first. Despite Phillip Hammond's fatuous comment that the 'British people did not vote to make themselves poorer', the economy did remarkably well in the seven months following the vote: "Retail sales are booming, manufacturing is expanding at its fastest rate in two and a half years, growth in the all-important service sector is at a 17-month high, and jobs creation remains impressive" (Warner, 2017: 2). Figures for April and May 2017 showed growth at 0.1 % and 0.5 % respectively, as compared with a fall in the 'Eurozone' economies, over the same period, of between 1.1% (Germany) and 7.5% (Ireland).

Gloomy scenarios continue to be peddled – presumably in the hope that increasing pressure will either slow down the pace of Brexit preparations, or bring them to a halt altogether. At very least, many of those making threats of moving their workforce out of the UK are trying to influence the government to go for a 'soft' as opposed to a 'hard' Brexit. For example, in October 2016, Goldman Sachs threatened to move just under 2,000 employees out the City of London if a 'hard' Brexit resulted in a loss of 'passporting rights' of employees in the Financial Services (FS) sector (Donnellan, 2016: B1).

'Passporting rights' means that UK FS companies can operate anywhere in the EU and EEA (which is the EU 28, in addition to Iceland, Lichtenstein, and Norway), and still be regulated by UK authorities. They can trade either by setting up 'branches' abroad (regulated under an 'establishment passport') or they can offer their services remotely, under the auspices of a 'services' passport (Protts, 2016). In effect this means that they have greater flexibility of operations, and are not subject to a host of different FS regulations in different markets. So to lose these might cause problems in terms of increased costs. However, as Warner (2016: 2) observes, 'passporting' is not the panacea that the FS would like to make out; he points out that the recognition of other countries' regulatory and supervisory standards ("equivalence") is a misconception, as:

"Large elements of finance are not covered by the agreement at all. Nor is equivalence something based on mutual recognition of each other's regulatory standards, or subject to legal arbitration of disputes, but is rather a political gift from the EU that can be withdrawn without explanation at 30 days notice."

If members of the banking community feel they have the economic 'clout' that allows them to make threats, they have misread the mood of the country. In the mind of the public, the banking sector is associated with exorbitantly high salaries, immense privilege, corruption – money 'laundering' and the Libor scandal (BBC, 2012b, Croft, 2016:17) – and was directly responsible for the 2009 economic recession. A counter-argument, designed to show how important the FS sector is to the UK economy, suggests that the major banks contribute large sums to the UK economy in terms of corporate tax. But just how true is this? In 2015, *The Independent* quoted an analysis of corporate tax returns undertaken by Reuters, which claimed that "...Morgan, Bank of America, Merrill Lynch, Deutsche Bank AG, Nomura Holding and Morgan Stanley all said their main UK arms paid no corporation tax" (Austin, 2015).

Similar accusations were made in January 2016, this time it was alleged that "...Lloyds Banking Group paid no UK corporation tax in 2014..." (Farand, 2016). In December of that same year, an article in *The Guardian* claimed that a report on FS tax contribution, published by the City of London Corporation and

PricewaterhouseCoopers (PwC), and detailing tax paid, was itself flawed. Sikka (2016) noted that:

"The report claims that the financial sector paid ... about £28.8bn (£71.4bn minus £42.6bn) in corporation tax, employers' NIC and business rates. However, none of this can be verified from the audited accounts of companies as they provide very little information about the taxes paid in the UK or elsewhere. A disclaimer buried in the fine print of the report says: 'PwC has not verified, validated, or audited the data and cannot therefore give any undertaking as to the accuracy of the study results.'"

So, the FS sector should tread carefully, as its threats are unlikely to have any resonance with the average UK voter. There is some evidence to suggest that certain members of the sector have already realised the impracticality of moving operations out of the UK, and are 'downsizing' their level of threat. Prior to the referendum, HSBC had warned that if the vote were won by the 'leavers', then the bank might relocate around one thousand jobs to France. By January 2017, the hard reality of relocation appeared to be taking its toll on the threat level, as in a statement to the Treasury Select Committee, the HSBC Chairman suggested that some FS firms (presumably including his own) "...may simply decide to cut jobs, rather than move roles elsewhere..." (Martin, 2017:3). To move jobs is neither easy, nor (as HSBC has obviously found out), cheap, and as such, despite the rhetoric it is likely that the FS sector will remain within the City of London.

2.2.4. Threats from Individuals

It was not just non-UK organisations that waded into the debate, but also high-profile individuals who should have known better. Witness the ill-judged intervention by US President Barak Obama – arguably the architect of the least effective US Foreign Policy in decades. On a farewell visit to David Cameron, Obama had the temerity to threaten the British public with dire consequences should they vote to leave the EU. In what the *Financial Times* described as a "... stinging rebuke to supporters of a British exit from the EU..." he threatened that, following a British exit, the UK would "...go to the back of the queue..." when seeking to develop new trade deals with the USA (Parker and Pickard, 2016).

It is interesting to speculate what his reaction would have been were a UK Prime Minister to threaten him about US relations with Canada and Mexico through the auspices of North American Free Trade Agreement (NAFTA). His intervention was not only arrogant, but also counter-productive, as it showed a remarkable lack of understanding of the British. To anyone with knowledge of the British character, it is obvious that we are a particularly obstinate nation, and to be threatened by a foreign leader into choosing a particular course of action, would be highly likely to result in the opposite choice being made. As the then-Culture Secretary John Wittingdale said in a pre-referendum interview with *The Daily Telegraph*: "I don't think the British people like leaders of other countries trying to bully them into doing something.[7] All of these things are part of a campaign to scare people into staying ..." (Swinford, 2016b: 13).

Obama's childish threats were soon overturned with the election to the US Presidency of Donald Trump; in December 2016, Wilbur Ross – who was to lead the new US foreign trade initiatives – is understood to have made "... securing a free trade deal between the US and Britain one of his top priorities..." (Riley-Smith, 2016c). Another high profile figure supporting 'remain' was Lord Henry Plumb, who in 2016 suggested that it would be "stupid" to leave the EU (Fredenburgh and Hart, 2016). What is perhaps not so widely known is that Plumb was an MEP, and later President of the European Commission – bearing in mind this pedigree, might he have been less than impartial in his assessment of the two options?

2.2.5. The Effect on Travel

The Chief Executive of Easyjet was quoted as having said that "...Brexit would raise the costs of foreign travel..." and that this would effectively mean that flying was 'reserved for the elite.' She claimed that "... British influence inside Brussels was essential to minimise disruption and administration between countries and keep down the cost of air travel" (Oltermann, 2016). She said: "How much you pay for your holiday really does depend on how much influence Britain has in Europe." Her argument was based around the supposition that: "As a result of Britain's membership [of the EU] the costs of flights have plummeted, while the range of destinations has soared. That's why Easyjet believes the benefits far outweigh the frustrations – and why the UK is better off as part of the EU" (Shipman and Evans, 2016:1).

Needless to say, she failed to produce any evidence for this assertion, aside from vague comments connected to the UK's ability to 'influence' the formation of travel legislation. It might have been more honest to have admitted that Easyjet is 'better off as a part of the EU' rather than attempt to suggest it was for the overall benefit of the nation. Furthermore, rather than the nebulous 'British influence' being responsible for the reduction in travel costs, it is more likely to have been a consequence of access to a multitude of routes within the EU, allied to reduced prices. Companies such as Easyjet have undoubtedly benefited from the SEM, but their 'success' has mostly been achieved through cost cutting initiatives, such as having few/no reserve aircraft available in the event of a flight

7. The last three foreign leaders who made this mistake were Adolf Hitler, Kaiser Wilhelm and Napoleon Bonaparte.

cancellation, making passengers check in on-line, print out their own boarding cards, pay for all 'extras' on board, and depart at unreasonable hours when take-off slots are cheaper. En passant, it is interesting to note that when it suits, Easyjet tries to hide behind the 'importance' of the EU in protecting passengers; yet this same company has been the subject of continued complaints from passengers who have tried (in line with EU directives) to get compensation for delayed or cancelled flights – in many cases to no avail. As Brignall and Tims (2015) noted, the airline's record of abiding by EU legislation is very poor, as a consequence of passenger:

"...compensation and other expense claims first ignored, and then fought at every stage – in the hope you'll give up and go away....Two months ago AirHelp, which provides online legal help for those claiming compensation for delays, said its data showed easyJet had the worst record of any airline for paying out what is legally due....Specialist lawyers describe how the company repeatedly puts in place legal obstacles to claims it says are perfectly legitimate. Since two major test cases went against the airlines earlier this year most carriers have been paying up without dispute – but not EasyJet."

2.2.6. Raising the Dead

As if the arguments put forward thus far had not been sufficient to demonstrate the desperation of the 'remainers', they resorted to putting words into the mouths of the dead. Taking two icons of middle-class, Conservative values (Winston Churchill and Margaret Thatcher), certain individuals sought to persuade voters that had these two Conservatives been alive they would have voted 'Remain' in the referendum. This serves as a classic example of how, with a subtle twist of historical facts, it is possible to make people who cannot answer back support a given opinion. In an interview with *The Sunday Times* (February 2016), Charles Powell – Margaret Thatcher's Chief of Staff – claimed that Thatcher would have "...gone along with..." the deal negotiated by Cameron, yet offered no evidence for this statement.

He went on to assert that: "There were certainly times as Prime Minister when her frustration with Europe boiled over. The one thing I never heard her propose was Britain's withdrawal from the EU." Whilst he may well be correct in this, it does not alter the fact that Thatcher was bitterly disappointed with the EU, and the covert federalist, centralist, and bureaucratic route it was pursuing. Lord Tebbit – probably Thatcher's closest Cabinet ally – commented that: "Attributing views to somebody who is dead in circumstances rather different to those in her lifetime is a very subjective matter" (Shipman et. al., 2016:1). Rather than speculate as to what Thatcher might or might not have said or done in a referendum that took place after her death, one only has to read her memoirs *The Downing Street Years* to gauge her attitude to the EU:

"...during my second term of office as Prime Minister certain harmful features and tendencies in the European Community started to become evident.... a more powerful Commission ambitious for power, an inclination towards bureaucratic rather than market solutions to economic problems and the re-emergence of a Franco-German axis with its own covert federalist and protectionist agenda.... the Community environment in which I had to operate became increasingly alien and frequently poisonous. The disputes were no longer about tactical or temporary issues but about the whole future direction of the Community....The Franco-German federalist project was wholeheartedly supported by a variety of different elements within the Community – by poorer southern countries who expected a substantial pay-off in exchange for its accomplishment; by northern businesses which hoped to foist their own high costs onto their competitors; by socialists because of the scope it offered for state intervention; by Christian Democrats whose political tradition was firmly corporatist; and, of course, by the Commission which saw itself as the nucleus of a supra-national government." (Thatcher, 1993: 727-728)

In April 2016, the 'remainers' disinterred another corpse and sent it into battle – this time it was that of Winston Churchill: David Cameron said that Churchill would have been a 'remainer' as he [Churchill] had "...argued passionately for western Europe to come together..." (*The Economist*, 2017a:35). This was doubtless in reference to the line in Churchill's 1946 speech in Zurich, in which he said that we must "...build a kind of United States of Europe."

However, the phrase 'kind of' is suggestive of something akin to, but not exactly the same as; critics have since argued over what exactly he meant by this, yet later in the same speech he implied that his model for Europe was based on that of the British Commonwealth: "There is already a natural grouping in the Western Hemisphere. We British have our own Commonwealth of Nations... and why should there not be a European group which could give a sense of enlarged patriotism and common citizenship to the distracted peoples of this mighty continent [Europe]?"[8]

Therefore, Cameron was quoting Churchill out of context, as have so many before and since. In his two most famous speeches on Europe (Zurich, September 1946 and the House of Parliament, May 1953) Churchill has been variously quoted correctly, quoted out of context, and mis-quoted – so much so that it is very difficult to know the truth. In saying this, Cameron had conveniently failed to mention that, as a parliamentarian and someone who opposed corruption

---

8. https://rm.coe.int/16806981f3

and tyranny, Churchill might well have at very least insisted on massive reform throughout the whole of the EU, and had he not got his way, he would have been likely to seek some form of alliance with the USA. As Churchill is supposed to have famously said in his Zurich speech of 19th September, 1946: "We are with Europe, but not of it." However, in the written record of this speech[9] there is no reference to him actually having said this, and many sources have instead attributed it to an article he wrote which was published in the *Saturday Evening Post* on 15th February 1930, in Philadelphia, USA. It was recycled again in a speech to the House of Commons, on 11th May, 1953, in which he outlined the UKs position towards Europe:

"Where do we stand? We are not members of the European Defence Community, nor do we intend to be merged in a Federal European system. We feel we have a special relation to both. This can be expressed by prepositions, by the preposition 'with' but not 'of' — we are with them, but not of them. We have our own Commonwealth and Empire" (*Hansard*, 1953:891).

What he actually said was more significant than what he has been misquoted as having said, as he made it quite clear that we do not intend 'to be merged in a Federal European system.' Roy Jenkins, in his excellent biography of Churchill[10], feels that despite what he may have said about Europe during WW2, Churchill was predominately focused on military concerns in the immediate post-war period (Jenkins, 2001:854). Churchill was used by Cowie (2016:3) to suggest an explanation for what he described as the "... disproportionate popularity amongst entrepreneurs..." of the 'leavers' amongst the population. The imagery of Churchill was employed shamelessly: a picture of the great man, under the headline: "Voting 'remain' could be our finest hour." Despite his enthusiasm for inter-European cooperation (a 'United States of Europe[11]'), Churchill is far better remembered for his speeches that opposed continental tyranny and oppression, and that celebrated Britain's willingness to stand alone against the Continental oppressor[12].

2.3. International Trade

International trade has been the subject of much speculation since it was known that the UK would have a referendum on continued EU membership. The basic difference between the EU and the UK is that whilst the UK wishes to continue

9. https://rm.coe.int/16806981f3
10. Jenkins, Roy. (2002). *Churchill: a Biography*. Plume; First Printing, Cover Torn edition (November 5, 2002)
11. Speech: Zurich (19th September 1946)
12. "We will fight on the beaches..." (May 1940); "... never before in the field of human conflict..." (August 1940).

operating in a single market, free from tariff barriers, the EU is split on the way forward. On one hand, the EU politicians want to ensure that the UK is punished for daring to leave the EU, and they feel that the best way of doing this is to deny British exports access to the SEM. By contrast, many EU exporters wish to continue trading with the UK without hindrance – ie. by simply extending the current trading regulations as they relate to the Single European Market (SEM) and the Customs Union (CU). In November 2016 Ilse Aigner, the Bavarian Economy Minister, publicly acknowledged that "Great Britain is one of the most important trading partners in Bavaria..." and commented that there "...must be ways to reestablish economic relations with Great Britain on a new basis without a break" (Hughes and Swinford, 2016:8).

This is also something that is desired by UK exporters. Any form of 'sanction' on the UK's future trading relations with the EU would be immensely damaging for both sides, but on balance, more so for EU exporters. One of the many 'scare' attempts relating to trade was made in October 2015, when thirteen former UK Ambassadors wrote an open letter to *The Sunday Times* in which they suggested that were we to leave, the task of setting up new trade agreements, claiming that "We would need to negotiate up to 50 new separate agreements to replace those we now have through the EU..." (Shipman, 2015:10).

Not long after this, in March 2016, David Cameron suggested that in the event of Brexit, the price of beef and lamb would increase, as "...British farmers could face tariffs of up to 70 per cent on produce sold in the EU after an Out vote" (Johnson, 2016:11). This may well be true, but it could only happen if the UK were to export to the EU, and such trade fell within the trading terms of the WTO. Furthermore, by the same logic, after we leave the EU, meat imported from the EU would also be subject to import tariffs, so UK farmers might take the opportunity to increase domestic sales (see Chapter 3.7. "Agriculture and Fisheries").

Cameron also challenged the 'out' voters to "...prove that the UK could retain access to the single market and explain whether the UK could continue to post border guards at Calais" (Holehouse, 2015a:4). This was a challenge without foundation, as he was hopefully aware – had he been unaware, then his claim to be competent to hold the highest political office in the UK would have been seriously compromised. To begin with, he must have understood that what he was asking was impossible: to leave the EU automatically implies that one has, at the same time, lost unfettered access to the Single European Market (SEM) and Customs Union (CU). Conversely, it could be argued that, taking his challenge at face value, the UK would always have access to the SEM, as even if it were not a member, it could still trade on WTO terms.

Secondly, the issue over the Calais border controls was a red herring, as Cameron must surely have been aware that the Calais-Dover border arrangements are controlled by the bi-lateral treaty of Le Touquet, and are without the jurisdiction of the EU. In an attempt to try and frustrate any 'post-Brexit' trade deals, the European Court of justice (ECJ) was said to be examining the feasibility of "...handing 38 national and regional parliaments the power to veto trade deals" (Stubbington, 2017:B1).

Were this to happen, then any deal relating to free trade between the EU and UK could be stopped by one vote – probably from a country that felt its economy was being threatened by the UK. Whilst the UK remains a member of the EU, individual countries do not have power of veto on trade deals, and cannot frustrate any UK trading activities; once we leave, such legislation would allow every nation to put its national interests before those of the group – a clear example of an attempt to stop the UK succeeding in trade in the future.

2.4. The Threat of War

In early 2015, Juncker had tried an emotional appeal to the British to remain by saying that 'Whoever does not believe in Europe, who doubts Europe, whoever despairs of Europe, should visit the military cemeteries in Europe.' His comments were seized on by Dr Liam Fox (a former defence secretary), who pointed out that: "The military cemeteries of Europe are testament to the failure of the continent to control extremism in the 20th century. Had Britain not been a free and independent nation, we would have been unable to intervene to protect Europe from the result of its own folly. Before we are lectured by the European Commission, we should take a look at the rise of extremism across the continent and ask whether they are helping or hurting" (Holehouse, 2015b:13).

Juncker's message was taken up one year later by David Cameron, who, on 9th May 2016 made one of the most outrageous, ill-informed, and provocative statements of the campaign, when he claimed that a vote to leave the EU could lead to Europe becoming involved in another war (Jenkins, 2016; Slack, 2016; Swinford, 2016e). Why this might happen he could not say, but as most European states are members of the mutual defensive organisation, the North Atlantic Treaty Organisation (NATO), his claim shows a remarkable lack of politico-military appreciation; perhaps it is just as well that he is no longer in charge of the country's destiny as he displayed a hyperbolically-hysterical understanding of what is a serious subject.

It is important to note that – internally – Europe has not been involved in wars since the end of WW2; since 2010 the only external threat to European peace and security has been the aggressive nationalism of Vladimir Putin's Russia in the Ukraine, when the Crimean peninsula was unilaterally occupied, and a separatist revolt encouraged in the East of the country. More recently, there have been accusations that Russia has sought to destabilise the West through hacking political party websites and other forms of cyber-interference in elections (Imeson, 2017), and poisoning Putin's opponents in the UK (Masters, 2018; Osborn, 2018).

The potential for further Russian aggression in the European Baltic states (Latvia, Lithuania, and Estonia), is currently being monitored by NATO, and as reported in *The Economist* (2016c:32), a recent study concluded that "... without a big new NATO presence in the Baltics, a Russian invasion force could reach Tallin (the capital of Estonia) and Riga (the capital of Latvia) within 60 hours." As a deterrent to Putin, NATO sent forces to carry out military exercises in some of the East European states that share borders with Russia. These measures to guarantee security have been NATO, not EU initiatives.

Brexit: KBO

CHAPTER 3 | THE FACTS OF EU MEMBERSHIP

3.1. Introduction

As previously observed, there has been much confusion and very little factual information on which to base a case for either staying or leaving the EU. So what are the facts relating to membership, and how might these have influenced voters had they been widely available at the time of the referendum?

3.2. EU Expansion

3.2.1. Introduction

The first of these facts is the constant expansion and realignment of purpose of the EU, all of which has taken place without any accountability on the part of the decision-makers towards the people they purport to represent, and has moved inexorably towards the establishment of a Federal Europe.

As Tylecote and Cash (2016:16) note: "The idea of a modern federal Europe was first seriously suggested by a Frenchman, foreign minister Aristide Briand, in 1929." Briand did not succeed, largely because WW2 intervened, and the immediate post-war priorities of Europe were the rejuvenation of devastated economies, and defence against the Soviet menace. The idea still held resonance with European politicians, however, and the first steps were taken towards the ultimate goal of federalism through the formation of the European Coal & Steel Community (ECSC) in July 1952.

Despite sounding as if it were a purely economic organisation, Jean Monnet (one of the 'founding fathers' of the EU), made it very clear that it was but a first step along the road to the political unification of Europe, in his speech to the National Press Club in Washington DC in April 1952. He explained that:

"L'établissement de la Communauté européenne du charbon et de l'acier jettera les bases d'une communauté de structure fédérale, gouvernée par des institutions communes, appliquant des règles communes, assurant à tous les mêmes droits et imposant à tous les mêmes obligations" (AEI, 1952:2).

("The establishment of the European Coal and Steel Community will be the foundations of a community of *federal structure*, governed by common institutions, applying common rules, ensuring the same rights and *imposing all the same obligations*") [author's italics]

Warming to his theme, Monnet also said in the same speech:

"L'établissement d'institutions et des règles communes assurant la fusion des souverainetés nationals unira les Européens sous une autorité commune et éliminera les causes fondementales des conflicts" (AEI, 1952:3).

("The establishment of common institutions and rules for the *merging of national sovereignties* will unite the Europeans under a common authority and will eliminate the fundamental causes of the conflicts") [author's italics]

Thus, from the very early days, those who formulated and executed EEC/EU policy had already identified a Federal Europe as their ultimate objective. What a pity, therefore, that instead of trying to achieve their goal through stealth and subterfuge, they had not been open and honest with the electorate right from the start.

At that time – post-war reconstruction, the emergence of the 'atomic age', worries over Soviet hegemony in Europe, and the spread of Chinese influence and the Korean War – the peoples of Europe might even have reacted positively to such an ambition. Instead, the population of Europe has been at best deliberately kept in the dark, and at worst lied to over some forty years: there have been gradual deliberately-planned changes in the EU's 'mission' for a number of years – all without the consent of the populous. The intention of key European leaders and bureaucrats is to ultimately arrive at a 'United States of Europe', underpinned with one currency (the Euro), and controlled through a myriad of Brussels-dictated regulations and requirements. To see this slide towards a Federal Europe, one only has to look at the path travelled since 1952, when the European Coal & Steel Community (ECSC) was formed.

The EU began life on 23rd July 1952 as the ECSC – a bloc that comprised Belgium, the Netherlands, France, Luxembourg and (the then) West Germany. The ECSC was the brainchild of the French politician Robert Schuman, who had proposed the creation of this industrial bloc a year earlier, to make war between historic rivals France and Germany "... not merely unthinkable, but materially impossible." This would be achieved by the "... pooling of coal and steel production ... [which] will change the destinies of those regions which have long been devoted to the manufacture of munitions of war, of which they have been the most constant victims."[1] ECSC subsequently developed into the EEC in March 1957, when it was presented as a group of countries that wished to trade

---

1. https://Europa.eu/European-union/about-eu/symbols/Europe-day/schuman-declaration_en

freely (without tariff or other trade barriers) – as expressed in Article 2 of the *Treaty of Rome* (1957). This treaty outlined the creation of a 'common market' between member states, based on the abolition of tariffs within this market, and a key element (in view of the political influence of French and German farmers), was the establishment of the Common Agricultural Policy (CAP).

In article 2 of the *Treaty*, it states that:

"The Community shall have as its task, by establishing a common market and progressively approximating the economic policies of Member States, to promote throughout the Community a harmonious development of economic activities, a continuous and balanced expansion, an increase in stability, an accelerated raising of the standards of living and closer relations between States belonging to it." (*Treaty of Rome*, 1957: 4)

However, the initial focus on economics and trade has changed radically since 1957, with an increased involvement in the socio-political fabric of the various member states – something that was never explained to many people who supported continued UK membership of the Common Market in the June 1975 referendum; many (the current author included) thought that they were validating membership of a free trade block, nothing else. The organisation has since 'developed' through a number of stages, each of which has taken it further away from a free trade bloc, and towards the invasive monolith of politico-social control which it now is. In 1992 we had the creation of the Single European Market (SEM) – one might have supposed, designed to reaffirm the whole purpose of tariff-less trade. Sadly, *The Cecchini Report* (1992), which presented the official stance of the EU towards the SEM, made it clear that the EEC was viewed as much more than a free trade organisation. The then President of the Commission, Jacques Delors, wrote a foreword to this report, in which he expanded on the 'social' dimension claiming that:

"The twelve Member States have rightly decided that it [the SEM] should be accompanied by policies that will lead to greater unity as well as more prosperity. They have therefore strengthened Community technology policies and enlarged the resources available for helping the long-term unemployed, youth unemployment and rural development; as well as the backward regions of the Community and those facing major restructuring problems." (Cecchini, 1992:xi)

Despite having no validation (such as an EU-wide referendum) for this decision to 'rightly decide' on deeper social integration, the route travelled took us to the *Maastricht Treaty* (November 1993); Tylecote and Cash (2016:118) identify this as a key moment in the development of the EU's federalist agenda, pointing out that it represented the transformation into a European Union. Despite this seismic change in relations between member states that the Maastricht Treaty entailed, the British public were still generally unaware that their independence had been signed away without consultation.

What makes it even worse, is the revelation by Tylecote and Cash (2016:125) that the politicians responsible for negotiations and signing, were apparently as ignorant of the implications of the *Treaty* as the people they should have represented. Following the signing of the *Treaty*, on February 7th, 1992, Foreign Secretary Douglas Hurd was said to have remarked: "...now we've signed it, we'd better read it." Whilst one might charitably assume that this was no more than an attempt at 'light-hearted banter', it does smack of 'gallows humour', and given the seriousness of the steps taken, and Hurd's position, it was highly inappropriate. He, at least, was in a position to read the *Treaty* in its entirety should he so desire; by contrast, the British public did not have that luxury.

Crucially, the word 'economic' was dropped – reflecting the organisation's increasing focus on 'social community', rather than free trade. There was a growing emphasis on 'social' projects (what Margaret Thatcher famously referred to as 'Socialism by the Back Door'), and greater harmonisation of socio-cultural policies, employment practices, international relations, and foreign aid. *Maastricht* was followed in November 2009 by the *Lisbon Treaty*, which effectively established a European Constitution. In their masterful study of the European project, entitled *The Great Deception: The Secret History of the European Union*, Christopher Booker and Richard North, suggest that this incremental development of the European 'project' was no accident, and that for a long time "... the project's founders..." had decided that "...its real nature and purpose should not be brought too obviously out into the open" (2003:1).

The 'real nature and purpose' of the European Project is the total political integration of the sovereign states of Europe into a European Federal 'Superstate', controlled by Brussels. Had they been aware of this from the outset, it is likely that the overwhelming majority of Europeans would have rejected this aspiration, as it will inevitably lead to a loss of cultural and historical identity, the right to have an independent outlook on world affairs, and a vertiginous growth in EU bureaucracy – paid for by an equally steep growth in financial contributions by member states. Even relatively recently-joined members have become disillusioned with the control exerted by Brussels. The Czech Republic joined in 2003, and yet only four years later, President Klaus said that despite his initially high expectations, the reality "...is worse than I expected. I expected Europe to be much more free, with much less government involvement, with less socialism" (Klaus, 2007:5).

3.2.2. The Trail of Treaties

In summary, the path to federalism can be charted through the various treaties signed since the 1950s – all without the approval of the various peoples they purport to represent:

1957 saw the creation of the European Economic Community (EEC), with the signing of *The Treaty of Rome.*

The Merger Treaty (1965), in which the three existing councils of Ministers (the European Economic Community [EEC], the European Coal and Steel Confederation [ECSC], and Euratom [European Atomic Energy Community]), were merged, and replaced by The European Council and the European Commission.

This was followed by *The Treaty Amending Certain Budgetary Provisions* (1970), which established a single budget for the EU.

In 1975, members signed *The Treaty Amending Certain Financial Provisions* (1975), which gave the European Parliament the right to reject the budget, and at the same time established a single Court of Auditors to monitor the EU accounts and financial management. This has proven highly contentious, as will become apparent later.

The *Single European Act* (1986): this was the first major reform of the treaties, and in response to growing disquiet over the lack of accountability, it introduced a system of qualified majority voting in the Council, in addition to increasing the role of the European Parliament, and widening the Community powers.

The Maastricht Treaty (1993): this was when the EEC was officially re-named as the European Union (EU), and it gave greater joint working (EU control) in matters of foreign policy, defence, police, and justice. Of major importance, *Mastricht* created economic and monetary union (the Euro), established the Single European Market, and introduced new policies relating to education and culture – all of which increased still further the powers of the European Parliament.

The Treaty of Amsterdam (1997): created an EU employment policy, and ensured greater cooperation in justice and home affairs – both of which fell under the jurisdiction of the EU.

The Treaty of Nice (2001): dealt with the composition of the Commission, in addition to the weighting of votes in the European Council, and the areas in which qualified majority voting was to be allowed.

The Treaty of Lisbon (2009): made sweeping reforms, aimed at making the EU "… more democratic, more transparent and more efficient" (BBC, 2011) – tacit recognition of the growing disquiet within the various national states of the perceived lack of accountability and transparency within the EU structures and Commissions. It followed an attempt (rejected by many national Parliaments) to impose a constitution on members – this would have represented a major step towards the establishment of a Federal Europe, but was too much for people to accept, and was rejected by the Dutch and French. The *Treaty of Lisbon* was very much a watered down version of the constitution, and was signed by all member states: it was presented as a treaty that 'streamlined' existing agreements, yet its critics claimed that it represented the 'federalisation' of Europe, through what was effectively a European constitution.

3.2.3. A Lack of Accountability

This ever-increasing emphasis on 'social' (rather than 'economic') considerations has reached worrying proportions, and begs the question whether the populations of Europe were aware of this change of emphasis, and the financial commitments this would entail? The likely answer is 'no', as most people would not have bothered to read the terms of the various Treaties that have moved us in this direction. In addition, as only one or two nations have been brave enough to put EU membership to the test in a national referendum, it could be argued that even had people been aware of these changes and had objected, they had little chance of preventing them happening. As it is highly unlikely that people were consulted as to their views on this change of direction at any point in the forty year progression, it is equally unlikely that these changes were enacted as a consequence of popular pressure from populations of member states.

Clark and Grimston (2012) struck a chord with most Britons when they suggested that many regard the EU as a "…bungling, overspending, interfering organisation whose tentacles need to be rapidly extracted from national life." As said previously, the ultimate objective of the EU leaders is to create a Federal Europe, governed from Brussels (and Strasbourg), and run by themselves and their appointed fellow-travellers. Evidence for this gradual move to a Federal Europe is to be found in the growing number of EU institutions that mirror those of national governments, and as EU law ultimately outranks national legislation (Swinford, 2016d), it is obvious that the EU institutions will eventually replace those of national governments. Taking just one area as an example, the EU has its own international representation through an organisation that most people will never have heard of: the European Union External Action Service. This organisation bases its legitimacy on the *Treaty of Lisbon*, and has: "...139 EU Delegations and Offices operating around the world, representing the European Union and its citizens globally."

These Delegations and Offices "...play a key role in presenting, explaining and implementing EU's foreign policies. They also analyse and report on the policies and developments of their host countries and conduct negotiations in accordance with given mandates." The EEAS summarise its activities as: "Maintaining political dialogue, administering development aid, overseeing EU trade issues and building cultural contacts..." (EEAS, 2016). The EU currently has diplomatic representation in 130 non-EU countries throughout the world.

It also has Ambassadors to twenty-six politico-commercial organisations, including The African Union (AU), The African, Caribbean and Pacific Group of States (ACP), The Andean Community (CA), The Association of Southeast Asian Nations (ASEAN), The Common Market for Eastern and Southern Africa (COMESA), The Council of Europe, The Economic Community of West African States (ECOWAS), The European Economic Area (EEA), The Gulf Cooperation Council (GCC), The League of Arab States (LAS), The Organisation for Economic Co-operation and Development (OECD), The Organisation for Security & Co-operation in Europe (OSCE), The Organisation of Eastern Caribbean States (OECS), The Organisation of Islamic Cooperation (OIC), The Southern African Development Community (SADC), and The World Trade Organisation (WTO).

In addition to this, it has four representatives to the United Nations stationed in New York, Geneva, Rome and Paris[2].

Why is all this highly-paid diplomatic representation necessary, particularly as it duplicates the representation of each member state? Surely the Ambassadors of each European State can represent their respective countries perfectly adequately, unless of course, the 'Big Brother from Brussels' is there to check that national ambassadors are toeing the EU Party Line? Furthermore, the EU has representatives to sixteen organisations described as 'Military and Civilian Missions and Operations', and supplies observers for general elections in many African countries. The EEAS is accused of pushing nations "...to shut down national embassies..." and use the money saved to justify an increase in its own budget which is increasingly profligate; in 2015 it was reported that the EEAS had ordered a dinner service for official functions – the estimated budget for this being £2-million; Conservative MEPs were scathing – as one observed: "If we need further confirmation of the pretensions and aspirations to grandeur of this organisation, this dinner service is it. It is absolutely appalling....we must put a scythe to the costs of the EEAS before it gets out of hand. We can no longer tolerate these false ambitions, not least when we are cutting back our own embassies" (Holehouse, 2015c:4).

---

2. https://eeas.Europa.eu/headquarters/headquarters-homepage/area/geo_en

There is an organisation that has potential for indoctrination of Europe's youth development: this is the Young European Ambassadors (YEA) programme, which recruits young people "...to represent the youth of their countries and network with young people from the European Union...". The YEA works under the EU Neighbours programme, aimed at establishing relations with Armenia, Azerbaijan, Belarus, Georgia, Moldova and Ukraine, and they "... exchange experience, discuss matters of direct concern to young people, share best practices and work together for a better future..." a somewhat nebulous and meaningless collection of platitudes.

The YEA website claims that "...Young European Ambassadors have been appointed for each Eastern Neighbourhood country and for the European Union Member States, including 'National Coordinators' for Armenia, Azerbaijan, Belarus, Georgia, Moldova and Ukraine. The National Coordinators are the main points of contact between the Young European Ambassadors of their country and the Network Coordinators, based in Brussels."[3] Most recently, Angela Merkel and eight other European Heads of State published a document in which they called for lessons in schools 'to nurture a European approach' and to 'tackle' Euroscepticism (Waterfield, 2014a: 15): this is a worrying development, as it shows the extent to which the EU will go to indoctrinate future generations as to the 'correct' way of thinking. The politicising of young people into a directed way of thinking has unfortunate precursors in the shape of organisations such as the Communist Youth League of China, the Komosol of the Soviet Union, the 'Falangistas' of Franco's Spain, and the Hitler Youth in Germany.

The growing emphasis on 'social' (as opposed to economic) considerations, has assumed alarming proportions. By 2010, it was claimed (again without a mandate from the electorate), that the EU's 'mission' was to:

- provide peace, prosperity and stability for its peoples
- overcome the divisions of the continent
- ensure that its peoples can live in safety
- promote balanced economic and social development
- meet the challenges of globalisation and preserve the diversity of the peoples of Europe
- uphold the values that Europeans share, such as sustainable development and a sound environment, respect for human rights and the social market economy[4]

The claim that one of the EU's missions is to 'overcome the divisions of the continent' is spurious. Assuming that 'divisions' relates to intra-European

3. http://www.euneighbours.eu/en/east/stay-informed/publications/young-European-ambassadors
4. http://www.Europa.eu/abc/12lessons

disputes, one is left wondering to what exactly they are referring, and how the EU has delivered against these objectives? In terms of disputes between member states and external entities, has the EU managed to solve the long-standing dispute between Greece and Turkey with regard to Cyprus? How has it solved friction between member states – such as between the UK and Spain caused by Gibraltar? What has it achieved at national level, such as the internal political divide that increasingly separates one region of Spain from another? This division has assumed even greater importance since the attempt by the Catalan government to hold an independence referendum on 1st October 2017, and the brutal suppression by Spanish national police (Guardia Civil) of people attempting to vote. It is telling that the EU refrained from comment on the behaviour of the Madrid government in ordering the police intervention.

One would have expected that an organisation that aspired to 'provide peace, prosperity and stability for its peoples', to 'ensure that its peoples can live in safety', and 'respect for human rights' would have been highly critical of such actions, yet the only comment from the EU was a statement that said: "Under the Spanish constitution, yesterday's vote was not legal..." (Strange and Crisp, 2017:12). This is ominous, as by extension one might assume that Brussels would condone a repeat of such violence under similar circumstances using the excuse that any actions taken to uphold a constitution were acceptable.

As the EU seems intent on devising a European constitution (without consultation with the peoples of Europe), one is left with the suspicion that the EU might adopt similar 'heavy-handed' tactics in defence of a 'Euro-constitution' and prevent any outward manifestation of dissent. The reason nothing critical of the violence was said is that the EU is terrified of any form of break-up within the Union – either at a national level (Brexit), or at a regional level – such as Catalunya and Scotland.

Given the long cultural, historical, political, and economic traditions of the nations that comprise the geographical continent of Europe, any attempt at European 'harmonisation' should take account of differences and values. Traders and diplomats have known this for centuries: the key is to understand the people with whom one is dealing, and to reach an amicable compromise when both sides are not in total agreement. Such an outcome means that both feel their point of view has been respected, and this reduces (perhaps eliminates) feelings of resentment. Thus, any attempt at European 'harmonisation' will always have to take account of national historical development, politico-economic goals, and the cultural values and attitudes that distinguish each nation. This is something that the EU does not appear to understand, despite the fact that the organisation has become the forum for contact and debate between nations that previously would have been unlikely to have worked closely together.

From Finland in the North, to Malta in the South, from Romania in the East to Ireland in the West, the EU project has grouped together a disparate number of countries with different cultures and distinct levels of politico-economic development. It could be concluded, therefore, that it is the EU itself that is the root cause of any resentment and dispute that may exist within Europe – as a consequence of its insistence on harmonisation and regulation of all aspects of life. This means imposing some form of order and/or regulation on countries in which such regulations may be perceived as unnecessary, and even threatening. It is the imposition of a 'one-size-fits-all' philosophy, coupled with a 'Nanny – State' attitude, which has led to growing resentment against the Brussels rule-makers who devise and then seek to impose these regulations. As Delhey (2007:257) in his study of trust within the EU acknowledges "... the European project involves handing over a good deal of national sovereignty to European bodies. This brings with it the risk of decisions being taken that are perceived to be against national interest." In this respect, if the EU had maintained its brief as a free-trade organisation, it would not now be concerned about 'divisions' within the continent.

The path to a Federal Europe must be trodden carefully and slowly, as any sudden move would alert the peoples of Europe as to what is happening. This is one of the reasons why the Brussels elite are so angry with the UK – we have seen this creeping federalism for what it is, have tried to stop it, and when this failed, we decided to leave – thus exposing the long-term objectives for all to see. The evidence shows that, for some fifty years, the leadership of the EU have consistently avoided telling the people they purport to represent what they are doing and why they are doing it. Furthermore, the situation is possibly even worse than appearances would suggest, as not only have the EU failed to tell the whole truth, but the President of the Commission (Juncker) has admitted to telling lies in relation to EU policy decisions. In 2011, he admitted that if things [topics of discussion] become serious "... we have to lie. The same applies to economic and monetary policy in the Union, I am very serious about it" (Pop, 2014). Nor is he apparently averse to physical violence when he does not get his own way having apparently threatened to "... punch a political journalist in the mouth" (Pancevski, 2017). If such accusations are true then they can only serve to undermine the credibility of Juncker, who has emerged as a bullying, lying politician, whose influence at the top of the EU brings nothing but shame on the so-called 'accountability' of EU functionaries, confirming the criticisms of those who complain about the lack of accountability of the European Commission in particular.

However, some supporters, rather than acknowledge the concerns raised in connection with the extent of EU control, have actually suggested that further integration is needed to "...save the EU..." claiming that for many "... continental Europeans, the core objective goes significantly beyond a free market. Common values, enshrined in the *Charter of Human Rights*, and social and environmental standards are essential, as is a supranational budget" (Goulard, 2016).

At last the truth has emerged, as such comments confirm the long-term objectives of many people (probably those with most to gain), and yet is an objective that has never been explicitly stated/explained to the electorate as a whole. This deception is what annoys many such as this author, who believe that such ideas and objectives should be a matter a public knowledge, not hidden and discussed amongst the self-appointed EU elites.

3.3. Paying for the EU

3.3.1. National Contributions

Probably the most contentious issue is that of contributions made by national governments to the EU budget, and the ways in which this money is spent on our behalf. There is considerable dispute over the correct figure relating to the UK's contribution; generally because such figures can be calculated in two ways – what is given to the EU by each country, and what is received by each country from the EU.

When receipts are deducted from contributions, the resulting amount is referred to as the net contribution. What, therefore, is the net contribution of each nation towards the EU budget? According to Wyatt (2016), the highest net contributors (ie. they give more than they receive) to the EU were:

Table 1: Net Contributors to EU (2016)	
Country	**Net Payment (€ billion)**
Netherlands	378
Sweden	270
Germany	219
Denmark	177
Finland	154
Austria	152
France	114
UK	110
Italy	85
Ireland	19
Total payments	**1,568**

Source: Wyatt (2016)

Perhaps surprisingly, the Netherlands is the largest net contributor, followed by Sweden and then Germany. In addition to the UK there are only nine other countries that are net contributors – which places a heavy financial burden on these nations, made all the more onerous by the wasteful way in which the budget is spent. Compared with the net contributors, there are nearly twice as many net beneficiaries:

Table 2: Net Beneficiaries from EU (2016)	
Country	**Net Receipt (€ billion)**
Luxembourg	2,760
Hungary	569
Lithuania	510
Greece	471
Malta	420
Latvia	396
Slovenia	368
Estonia	355
Portugal	355
Czech Republic	273
Bulgaria	248
Romania	225
Slovakia	175
Belgium	162
Cyprus	131
Croatia	36
Spain	9
Total receipts	**7,463**

Source: Wyatt (2016)

As can be seen, even on this crude comparator, the 'outgoings' (€7,463-billion) considerably exceed the 'incomings' (€1,568-billion), and even when the UK contribution is factored in (€110-billion), this still only gives a budget of giving a total budget of some €1,668-billion, and outgoings still dwarf incomings – which suggests that the EU will either have to curtail expenditure, or increase revenue in the near future. If they were to lose the net UK contribution, the situation would be suddenly made much worse, and much more quickly.

Whilst we can bandy figures around, the real problem as far as the rest of the EU is concerned, is that following Brexit, the UK's contribution will have to be paid by other countries. The countries that are most likely to have to pay the UK's share of the budget will most probably be those that are already major net contributors: *viz.* probably Germany, France, Italy, the Netherlands, Sweden, and Denmark. It is, therefore, no surprise that Germany is leading the demands that the UK pay a hefty 'divorce bill' – presumably in the hope that this will delay any increase in payments at least in the short term. When compared to the net contributions of other Member states, the role and importance of the UK becomes apparent; Silvia Amaro (Digital Reporter for CNBC), pointed out that: "Britain's exit from the European Union means that one of the bloc's biggest economies will stop making contributions to its budget. This raises questions as to how long the U.K. will continue to pay its share of the budget and how can the EU fill the gap once Britain has officially left" (Amaro, 2018). It is this question that has preoccupied the EU bureaucracy ever since it became clear that the UK was to leave.

The problem for the EU is that these countries all have growing anti-EU parties, many of which are vociferous in their condemnation of EU profligate expenditure, and could be expected to oppose taking over all, or part of the UK's contribution. This would undoubtedly hit the EU hard, perhaps even leading to its break-up, which is something that is viewed with horror by those organisations that regard the EU as providing a stable platform for high-powered (and well-paid) jobs, and global politico-economic influence.

In addition to objections as to the sheer size of the budget and member state obligations to this, there are serious and sustained objections to the way in which this money is spent, and the lack of accountability of finances. For example, in October 2012 the Ford motor vehicle company announced that it was to cut hundreds of jobs in the UK, as a consequence of moving its 'Transit' van production plant to Turkey. Manufacturing in Turkey had become a more attractive proposition for many reasons, principally as the Turkish plant had recently undergone a programme of modernisation – using a loan of £452-million, provided by the European Investment Bank (Grew and Hookham, 2012). European taxpayer's money was effectively being used to move jobs away from the UK towards a non-EU competitor country!

3.3.2. EU Salaries

A major reason why membership of the EU is so expensive is that a large proportion of the money given by national governments is used to pay the salaries of EU officials, and Members of the European Parliament (MEPs). Member states make a contribution based on a percentage of their Gross National Income (GNI) – effectively meaning that the more successful they are, the more they pay. Conversely, if their GDP is comparatively low, they pay relatively less; the contribution made by member states, whilst initially 'designed as a balancing item' has, in the Commission's own words "... become the largest source of revenue" (EU Budget, 2017). Other sources include revenues from customs duties, agricultural levies, revenues from VAT receipts, and fines imposed on large companies for one reason or another. In 2011, the budget was 141.9 billion; in October 2016, the budget for the next financial year (2016-2017) was estimated to be €161.8-billion (Geier, 2016). Geier is the MEP who will negotiate on behalf of the Parliament for the bulk of the new budget, setting out requirements for the immediate future.

There are other budgetary considerations, such as the UK's rebate: in 1984, Prime Minister Margaret Thatcher secured a UK contribution rebate, based largely on the terms of the Common Agricultural Policy (CAP). Prior to 1984 approximately 80% of the EU budget went on farming subsidies, mostly to French, German, and Italian farmers, allowing them to maintain their largely uneconomic agricultural practices. By 2009, largely as a consequence of Thatcher's intervention, the amount dedicated to the CAP had fallen to around 41% of the total budget.[5] In addition, there are other factors, such as the lump sum payments to Denmark, the Netherlands, Sweden and Austria. The real problem is that EU budgets are set according to what is required in terms of expenditure – not what is available. If more money is needed, then the solution is to increase the contributions of member states.

Unlike most ethically-driven and law-abiding businesses, the EU has proven itself incapable of maintaining good budgetary control – possibly because the people who spend this money are unaccountable for their decisions to the electorate. In November 2012, Austria, the Czech Republic, Germany, the Netherlands, and the UK, wanted a cut in EU expenditure, pointing out that as national governments had been forced to make cuts in their levels of national expenditure, the EU should do likewise. Somewhat predictably, then EU Budget Commissioner countered this suggestion by saying that there could not be "… more Europe with less money" (Grimston, 2012). He obviously did not realise that many people might actually want less Europe with less money!

This admirably illustrates the divide between the well-paid, upper-middle class Brussels bureaucrats and the vast majority of the general European public – most of whom do not have the benefit of exorbitant salaries, guaranteed index-lined pensions, and profligate expense accounts. The state of the chaos surrounding EU finances is best illustrated by the fact that the EU- appointed auditors refused to sign off the EU financial accounts for 2011: Waterfield (2012) says that was due to "… breaches of public procurement rules, ineligible or incorrect calculation costs claimed to the EU co-financed projects or over – declaration of land by farmers." He claims that the auditors discovered some four billion Euros' worth of 'material errors.' Is it any wonder that the EU is regarded as incompetent and/or corrupt? In addition to the expenditure on EU- funded 'projects', there is the issue of salaries. According to Richard Corbett, Labour MEP for Yorkshire and Humber, the average MEP earns around €75,000 per annum (Corbett, 2016), for a basic

---

5. http://Europarl.Europa.eu/.

37 hour week. There are 751 elected MEPs, which based on the average salary as presented by Corbett, costs EU taxpayers around €56,325,000 per annum (some £51 million). This rather begs the question whether so many MEPs are needed, as each country they represent also has its own elected parliament. President of The Commission, Juncker reportedly earns £245,629, in addition to a 'residential allowance' of £36,844, and a monthly expense allowance (no receipts needed) of £1,135. When he eventually retires, he can look forward to a pension of £52,500 per annum (Midgley, 2016).

In addition to this expense, there is the unnecessary cost of moving the European Parliament between Brussels and Strasbourg twice a year, to allow for accommodation in its two homes, at an estimated to cost £1.4 billion a year (Clark and Grimston, 2012) – basically to allow for the national sensibilities of the French. In 2012 *The Sunday Times* reported that, in addition to their salaries, EU officials receive a 16% bonus if they work outside their country of origin – presumably to offset the hardships endured when working in Brussels and Strasbourg! For EU Ambassadors – stationed in any one of the 130 EU embassies around the world, this hardship allowance could be up to 40% of their salary – as in India (Pancevski, 2012:6). All officials are entitled to eighteen days paid holiday a year, in addition to "Europe Day", an annual celebration of 'peace and unity' in Europe. Even this appears to provide not one, but two holidays, as it is celebrated on 5th May for the Council of Europe, and 9th May for the EU. It is highly likely that most UK citizens will have never even heard of this, created in 1964 in honour of one of the founding fathers of the EU – French politician Robert Schumann – and it is not a national holiday for most citizens of member countries, who have to continue working to pay for this nonsense.

3.3.3. EU Expenses

All of these salaries and perks are supplemented by 'expenses', which can be considerable, especially as they apparently remain largely unchecked: "Nearly all MEP's claim their entire expenses allowance, because European Union officials insist it would be too costly to ask for receipts" (Holehouse, 2016b:15). This has led to widespread abuse, just as the case of the Labour MEP Peter Skinner, who, according to Holehouse (2016b:15), was convicted of fraud, as he "…used staffing expenses to pay his divorce settlement…"

As reported in *The Daily Telegraph* recently it took three years and 190 requests for information to get the EU to provide a list of expenses claims by staff, and then Helen Darbishire (Executive Director of 'Access Info Europe') was only given data relating to two months in 2016. In this, Juncker is reported to have claimed €29,900 (around £22,610) in this two month period, including "…€700 in daily allowances and more than €1,664 on accommodation. By far his most expensive

trip was an official visit to Rome in late February [2016] which cost €19,395..."
Even this was dwarfed by the expenses claim submitted for the same period by
Federica Mogherini, in her role as 'High Representative of the EU for Foreign
Affairs and Security Policy, and Vice-President of the European Commission' –
she claimed €100,749 (Swinford, 2017c: 4-5).

This profligate expenditure is paid for by tax payers from the various EU
countries, only to have them frittered away on dubious expenditures. This is
a major reason why many people feel the system needs reforming – but that
will never happen as long as the likes of Juncker are still accruing personal
benefit from the EU. *The Daily Telegraph* (Editorial, 2017d:15) summed up
the situation admirably: "No wonder cynical Britons are determined to stop
financing this jamboree any longer, and [are] concerned that they may be
lumbered with costs like these by being presented with an inflated, unfair
Brexit bill."

3.4. The Free Movement of People

3.4.1. Introduction

One of the basic tenets of the EU is the 'free movement of people.' Whilst this
might seem to present equality of opportunity throughout the EU, the reality is
somewhat different. Nobody appears to have questioned why the EU felt this
was such an important policy, and why they insist on it remaining part of the
Brexit negotiations. High levels of unemployment create significant problems
for governments, which have an economic and social duty to care for them. This
costs money, and in the long run, contributes to levels of disaffection in society,
and can result in social problems and even the breakdown of society: this is
why the freedom of movement policy is vital for many EU countries, as if the
unemployed can be encouraged to go abroad to seek work, then the problem
(and governmental responsibility) is lessened.

The group that is most likely to have few or no family ties in their own
country, to be socially (and internationally) mobile, to be motivated to look for
employment opportunities outside their country of origin, and who have (or can
acquire) language skills for working abroad, are those aged between 16 and 25.
Since the economic crisis of 2009, unemployment in EU countries has rocketed,
especially amongst those aged under twenty-five. People in this age bracket are
generally far more likely to travel to look for work, and the 'free movement of
people' policy encourages them to do just this, especially as youth unemployment
has reached dangerous proportions in many EU nations – principally those in
Southern Europe.

3.4.2. Youth Unemployment in the EU

The countries with the highest levels of youth unemployment are the Mediterranean countries, such as Greece, Spain, and Italy – with Greece and Spain being by far the worst. Figures from Eurostat (the EU's official statistics guide), shows that for 2016, youth unemployment (as defined by those aged 16-25) was as follows:

Table 3: Youth Unemployment (2016)	
Country	Average Percentage of Youth Unemployed
Greece	47.3
Spain	44.4
Italy	37.8
Croatia	31.1
Cyprus	29.1
Portugal	28.2
France	24.6
Slovakia	22.2
Finland	21.1
Romania	20.6
Belgium	20.1
Luxembourg	19.2
Sweden	18.9
Poland	17.7
Latvia	17.3
Ireland	17.2
Bulgaria	17.2
Slovenia	15.2
Lithuania	14.5
Estonia	13.4
United Kingdom	13.0
Hungary	12.9
Denmark	12.0
Czech Republic	10.5
Austria	11.2
Malta	11.1
Netherlands	10.8
Germany	7.0

Source: EurosTAT (2017)

This explains why there is an influx of foreigners looking for work in countries with lower levels of youth unemployment, such as Germany, the Netherlands, and the UK – in the case of the latter, many migrants find it easier to secure employment in this country as most have been taught English in school. The other way around – UK citizens seeking work abroad – does happen, but on a very much smaller scale, partly due to the language barrier, but mostly due to the higher levels of unemployment that exist in many countries of the EU.

Under the EU freedom of movement regulations, all citizens are entitled to live in the country of their choice, which eliminates many potential socio-economic problems for those countries with high levels of youth unemployment. Whilst this might be regarded as a good thing by the EU in general, and countries such as Spain and Greece in particular, it is not viewed in such a favourable light by the native populations of the countries targeted as destinations, and the issue of unrestricted immigration was a key reason why people voted 'leave' in the referendum, in the hope of regaining control of our borders. Not all sectors of UK society have been affected by immigration to the same extent. In areas, such as Clacton in Essex (an area that registered a high 'leave' vote 57,447 as opposed to 25,210 for 'remain')[6], where much of the electorate come from poorer, working class backgrounds, is typical of the areas Nigel Farage was referring to when he said that it is the working class who are most "...affected by crime and mass immigration driving wages down" (Pickard, 2014:2).

3.5. The Legal Minefield

A country relies on its legal system to maintain law and order, and for this the legal system to be objectively interpreted by an independent judiciary. The problem is that in joining the EU, states are subject to European interpretation of the law, even though it may be contrary to the law of an individual nation. We have been consistently promised that UK law will still function, yet just two months before the referendum the government quietly published a report on the legal position of UK courts with regard to the European Court of Justice (ECJ) – the EU's attempt to bring all of Europe under one legal system. In this report, Swinford (2016d) notes that the government acknowledges the fact that: "Britain is 'obliged' to accept European Union laws and judgments, according to an official report slipped out by ministers ahead of the formal start of the referendum campaign. The 96-page paper, which was published without fanfare ... highlights the fact that Britain has to adopt EU law and accept the rulings of the European Court of Justice." Furthermore, the report makes it clear that:

"Member states have to make sure that any actions they take are consistent with the rules in EU law, and must adopt any legislation necessary to give effect to EU law in their national law. The National Courts share responsibility for enforcing

6. EU Referendum (2017) *"European Union (EU) Referendum Results"*. http://www.tendringdc. gov.uk/council/elections-voting/European-union-eu-referendum

EU law with the European Court of Justice. Any person or company has a right to take the UK Government (or in some cases another person or company) to a UK court for failure to comply with EU law. Where a domestic court finds that someone has breached EU law, it will take the necessary steps to ensure EU law is given effect, which may include disapplying national legislation that conflicts with it."[7]

As Michael Howard – a former Leader of the UK Conservative Party, and a Queen's Council – noted, rather than Parliament being sovereign in forming legislation, and this being interpreted by British Courts, the European Court of Justice (ECJ) "... now routinely interferes in the most fundamental duties of an elected government" (Howard and Aikens, 2016). Areas in which it has interfered include 'Health Policy', 'Price Control' (especially with regard to the sale of alcohol and tobacco), 'Social and Labour Policy' (working hours etc.), 'Utility Regulation' (gas, water, electricity, telecommunications), 'Fisheries Policy', and 'Airport Regulation' – all of which do require legislation, but which can be discussed in the UK Parliament, and then implemented (or not) as MPs see fit.

There is no need to have such minutiae of detail discussed and then imposed by the European Parliament, backed by the ECJ. With regard to landing rights at airports, for example, Pitt (2016) observes that "...when the UK government negotiated rights to increase the number of flights between Delhi and London, the UK government was unable to offer some slots at Heathrow to Indian airlines, whereas the Indian government was able to do the same in reverse at Delhi and Mumbai." This was a direct consequence of EU interference, which issued EU Slot Regulation 93/95 (amended in 2004); this regulation "...lays down the terms on which slots should be allocated to air carriers, when they can transfer slots between themselves and when they might lose the right to slots for the next scheduling season." Why should the EU concern itself with such detail is anybody's guess, other than the fact that it (and hundreds of other EU 'Regulations') keep hundreds of 'Eurocrats' in lucrative employment.

The ECJ should not be confused with the European Court of Human Rights (ECHR[8]) which is a European (as opposed to an EU) organisation; it is, however, the Court of Law of the EU with which it has very strong links, and both work closely together. It is fair to say that the EU in general and the ECJ in particular, play an influential role in the ECHR. This is important, as it represents another area in which UK law is being undermined, this time from Strasbourg, but undoubtedly as a part of a long-term strategy that has the support of the EU. Notwithstanding

7. http://www.telegraph.co.uk/news/2016/04/14/uk-obliged-judgments-of-European-courts-official-document-from-m/
8. https://www.equalityhumanrights.com/en/what-are-human-rights/how-are-your-rights-protected/what-European-court-human-rights

this technical difference, both the ECJ and the ECHR are increasingly accused of supporting offenders, rather than focusing on the victims of crime. For example, in February 2011, the ECHR reportedly ruled that the UK could not prevent those serving jail sentences from voting as this infringed their 'human rights.' In the same year, it prevented a Nigerian rapist from being deported as this would 'violate his right to a family life.'

However, even by the convoluted logic by which the ECHR operates, such a ruling does not make sense, for, as Doyle and Warren (2011) point out, the man had no wife, "... long-term partner or children in the UK – factors which foreign criminals have used to stay here under Article 8 of the Human Rights Act." The panel of seven judges "...including judges from Bosnia, Albania and Montenegro – said the court must protect his 'social ties' with Britain, which have grown while he resisted deportation."

So in other words, had the UK authorities deported him immediately he could not have used this spurious defence. All of which rather suggests that to prevent ECHR interference, justice should be carried out as swiftly as UK law permits. Naturally such a perverse ruling led to considerable protest, but to little avail, as when he was Prime Minister Tony Blair signed the Human Rights act in 1999, committing the UK to abide by the ECHR's decisions. This was frustrating for Mrs May when she was Home Secretary to extradite the 'hate preacher' Abu Qatada (Hope, 2017), prior to this, the other such preacher (Abu Hamza) had been eventually deported, but following his incarceration in the USA, a lawyer at the ECJ ruled that Abu Hamza's daughter-in-law had a legal right to stay in the UK, as to deport her would deprive her son (a British citizen) of his right to a family life (Barrett and Whitehead, 2016:6).

Their deportations were blocked by the ECJ and ECHR for up to a decade, and the legal battles cost the UK taxpayer millions of pounds. This led to a storm of protest, which was equaled only by the ECHR's 2013 ruling that sentencing convicted murderers to imprisonment for the remainder of their natural life was a breach of their human rights (Barrett, 2013). Linked to this is the case of the European Arrest warrants (EAW), which has attracted serious criticism from senior legal figures, in particular with regard to EU extradition laws (Leppard, 2012). Ungoed-Thomas and Follain (2011) claimed that: "Almost half of the human rights judges at Strasbourg who are routinely overturning the decisions of [UK] parliament and Britain's highest courts had no judicial experience before their appointment."

3.6 Foreign Trade

3.6.1. Introduction

In terms of international trade, the EU controls all external relations outside the EU area on behalf of all member states as part of the drive towards 'harmonisation.' This means that EU member states have lost the right to enter into bilateral trading agreements outside the trade bloc. This latter point is crucial to the development of post-Brexit international trade, and yet is something that many people only began to realise in the pre-Referendum discussions. Any state wishing to trade with a non-EU country must undertake negotiations via the Brussels machinery, and any subsequent agreement must be ratified by all member states – not by a simple majority.Since 1973, all UK country-to-country trade deals have been handled by EU trade specialists on behalf of all EU member states: meaning that no single country has been allowed to negotiate separate trade deals with a non-EU state.

In effect this has meant that UK businesses wishing to enter new overseas markets have had to abide by agreements decided by the Brussels bureaucratic machinery, which has had the effect of reducing the flexibility of terms and conditions that UK business might be able to offer, thus reducing the country's international competitiveness. No 'imbalance' in terms of non-EU trading is allowed, which makes for a blunt, highly-bureaucratic, and exceeding slow process of negotiation: the consequence of which makes the EU uncompetitive in international terms (Levy, 2012), and excessively slow in the ratification of agreements. Indeed, the recent trade agreement with Canada was seven years in the making, and was almost stopped at the last minute due to a refusal of the regional government of the Belgian state of Wallonia to agree with their national parliament (Beesley, 2016; Rankin, 2016b).

Furthermore, as a consequence of forty years of central control over international trade deals, many government departments have little or no experience of negotiating without the confines laid down by Brussels (MacLellan, 2016; Reuters, 2016; Spence, 2016); which means that the UK government has to now re-learn most of what it once knew in relation to international trade negotiations.

3.6.2. Current UK/EU Trade

As can be seen in table 4 overleaf, figures for 2016 (the latest available) show a healthy EU-UK trade, and most businesses are loath to jeopardise this:

Table 4: Top UK/EU Export/Imports (2016)			
Export Destination	Value (US $ billion)	Import Source	Value (US $ billion)
Germany	43.6	Germany	46.5
France	25.9	France	27.0
Netherlands	25.6	Netherlands	26.6
Ireland	22.9	Ireland	25.5
Belgium	15.8	Belgium	17.8
Italy	13.1	Spain	13.1
Spain	12.7	Italy	12.9
Export value	**159.6**	**Import Value**	**169.40**

Source: based on Workman (2017) http://www.worldstopexports.com/united-kingdoms-top-import-partners/; http://www.sowoll.com/en/blog/post/137-united-kingdom-s-top-import-partners

In 2016 the top seven (in terms of trade) EU nations sold us some $9.8 billion's worth more than we sold them. This trade deficit with the EU has been getting worse over the past five years or so, with the UK selling far less to Europe in general (and the EU in particular) than it buys. Normally, this negative balance of payments (BOP) would be considered undesirable, but if no UK-EU free trade deal is reached, then we would have to trade under WTO rules – the most important of which would be a reversion to tariff barriers and product specifications on goods imported.

Under such circumstances, a trade imbalance might prove a negotiating advantage, as tariff barriers are mutually applicable, so were the current imbalance to remain, then EU exporters to the UK would lose more – collectively – than would UK exporters to the EU. So, from the point of view of Brexit, this negative BOP actually strengthens the UK's negotiating stance: at very least, it must certainly make EU exporters think very carefully about future trade with the UK. As observed earlier, if post-Brexit trade were to operate on WTO regulations (i.e. import tariffs), the EU as a whole would be worse off to the tune of some $10 billion; furthermore, most of this would hit the nations featured in the table above, with the exception of Italy, to where we export more than we import.

Despite the much – trumpeted advantages of being part of a free trade bloc, this does not appear to have had a positive effect on the UK trade balance with the EU. However, as Elliott (2016) points out: "Figures from the ONS (2018) showed that Europe is gradually becoming a less important destination for UK companies. In 2000, 60% of exports went to other EU countries, but the percentage fell to 58% in 2005, 54% in 2010 and 47% in 2015." An analysis of trade figures shows a long – term decline in the importance of the EU as a trading partner from 1999 to 2015. Thus, at a strategic level, the EU is becoming less important as a trade partner – despite the stance of many politicians who continue to stress the importance of the EU as the key trading partner, when in fact it is the USA – with which we had a huge trading surplus of nearly £40-billion in 2015 (Burton and Salmon, 2017).

Those who would argue that the EU's share of UK trade is too large and important to lose, are looking at an artificially – created situation: quite naturally UK businesses have focused on the EU, as EU and UK government legislation has done everything possible over the last forty years to encourage such a relationship – generally at the expense of our global position. Brexit has given us the opportunity to reverse this process, and once more become a truly global trading nation. Table 6 (see below) shows that China, for example, only accounts for $18 billion's worth of our exports, yet it has the largest population in the world. Surely there must be considerable opportunities for UK exporters in the Chinese market?

3.6.3. The 'Rotterdam Effect'

When examining the macro – level trade flows with the EU, there is an additional consideration: that of the so-called "Rotterdam Effect": this refers to a major trade anomaly in which, othose UK goods that are sent to the EU, many go no further than Rotterdam in the Netherlands, from where fifty percent shipped other non-EU destinations.

So whilst technically such goods are exported to the EU, many are not actually soldwithin the EU. This is why the Netherlands features as one of the top five export markets, rather than the fact that the Dutch have an overwhelming desire for British-made produce. explained by UK Trade (a publication of the Office for National Statistics):

"The Rotterdam effect is the theory that trade in goods with the Netherlands is artificially inflated by those goods dispatched from or arriving in Rotterdam despite the ultimate destination or country of origin being located elsewhere. Some commentators feel that the Rotterdam effect distorts the UK's trade relationship with EU and non-EU countries. For example, oil exported from Saudi Arabia to Rotterdam and re-exported to the UK (possibly without processing) may be counted as an EU import rather than a non-EU import. Conversely, a product exported by the UK to Rotterdam and subsequently transited to a non-EU country may be counted as an export to the EU rather than the rest of the world" (ONS, 2015).

Based on the argument presented above, one has to ask why there has been so much opposition to the idea of continued free trade once the UK leaves the SEM, and why did the EU and other non-UK institutions in particular, use trade to try to coerce the British public into voting 'remain'? The problem lies not with businesses from within the EU, but the EU institutions themselves. As will become apparent later (Chapter 5: "Brexit Contagion"), it is the EU that is vehemently opposed to giving the UK continued access to the SEM after 29th March, 2019, as if the UK can leave the EU and still maintain preferential trading rights, then what is to stop other countries from doing the same? If this happened, there would be the potential for a collapse of the whole EU infrastructure and institutions, with a consequent loss of many highly-paid jobs and personal influence, not to mention lucrative expense accounts.

Ironically, it could even mean that the EU would be forced to revert to being a group of countries that trade freely between each other – what we were apparently promised back in the early 1970s. If, in the short-to-medium term at least, trade is to be conducted on a tariff basis for political, rather than trading reasons, then ironically it is likely to provide further ammunition for continental Eurosceptic parties to pressure their respective governments to hold referendums on their continued membership. Either way, Brussels has painted itself into a very tight corner, within which it has limited room for manoeuver.

Worryingly for the EU, a growing number of developing nations are using the UK's imminent departure as a reason to refuse to sign trade agreements with the EU. Academics from the Overseas Development Institute have cited the example of the proposed deal between Brussels and the East African Community (EAC) group, which has already been rejected by Tanzania as a consequence of "... the 'turmoil' engulfing the EU following the Brexit vote and the skewed terms of the agreement..." It is suggested that many more countries will follow suit over the next two years; if they wish to trade with the UK on their own terms they cannot afford to be locked into the Brussels straightjacket of negotiations (Gutteridge, 2016b). From the point of view of Brussels, the sooner the 'turmoil' abates, the better; this suggests that the 'doom-laden' scenarios currently being discussed – such as the ten years to do a trade deal predicted by the ex-UK Ambassador to the EU, Sir Ivan Rogers (Henley and Roberts, 2016; Keunssberg, 2016), are unlikely to come to fruition.

3.7. Agriculture and Fisheries

3.7.1. Agriculture

Although the percentage of the annual budget allocated to the Common Agricultural Policy (CAP) has declined over the years, it is still significant and as such remains an area of contention. The CAP accounted for some 74% of EU expenditure in 1985, but by 2015 this had been reduced to 39% (CAP, 2017) – largely as a consequence of pressure from the UK, and in particular, Prime Minister Margaret Thatcher. The addition of around nine million poor farmers from the newly-joined countries of Eastern Europe, brought new problems and demands on the budget, causing many to question the way in which funds are allocated; as Mann (2002:15) observed, the Dutch proposed that much of the farming aid budget be transferred away from farmers in the West of Europe, to the poorer farmers from the East.

It is unlikely, however, that such a proposal would ever be accepted as the French, Spanish, Greek, Portuguese, and Italian economies are heavily reliant on the CAP subsidies. In 2005, the USA offered to cut farming subsidies bilaterally – meaning that both they and the EU would cut the subsidy payments given to their respective farming communities. This offer was dismissed out of hand by the then-French Interior Minister, Nicolas Sarkozy who, according to Arnold *et. al.* (2005) 'unleashed a "tirade" against the proposals.' In France, the farming community (and farming-related industries) represent a sizeable proportion of the electorate, so agreeing to cut the subsidies they receive would have been tantamount to committing political suicide.

3.7.2. Fisheries

The EU Common Fisheries policy (CFP) is possibly even more contentious than the CAP: according to critics has resulted in small-scale fishermen suffering as a consequence of larger foreign vessels that have access to UK fishing grounds (Rigby, et al, 2013:6). According to the Institute for Government[9] there are two main areas that constitute the CFP: 1) Fisheries management, 2) International Policy and Co-operation. Catches are regulated by the quota system – a particular *bête noir* of UK fishermen, as it means that any boat accidentally catching more than its allotted quota has to return the 'extra' catch to the sea. Consequently, many fish are returned dead, as there is insufficient time between catching and evaluating what has been caught, before the fish die. Therefore, the quota system does not prevent over-fishing, or even the catching of undersized fish: all it does is ensure that many dead fish are discarded. The madness does not stop here, however, as the EU gives

---

9. https://www.instituteforgovernment.org.uk/explainers/common-fisheries-policy

fishing subsidies of around £20-million a year to Austria, Hungary, Slovakia, and the Czech Republic – none of which have a coastline (Gillespie, 2011). An editorial in *The Scotsman* (2004) estimated that nearly:

"..£200-million of European funding will be pumped into the fishing industries of the European Union's ten new member states, despite the fact that three of them are landlocked... at a time when part of Scotland's fishing industry is being decommissioned, Hungary, the Czech Republic and Slovakia will all share in the hand-out. Ted Brocklebank, the fisheries spokesman for the Scottish Tories, said the payments, which can be spent on modernising port facilities and investment in processing, proved it was time for the UK to pull out of the Common Fisheries Policy (CFP). 'While we are being told that our fleet must contract because there are too many boats chasing too few fish, the great lie about what's really going on has finally been exposed,' Mr Brocklebank said. 'While we are being forced to decommission our fleet, the new accession states are being funded to modernise theirs.'"

The Brussels-imposed CFP has meant that the UK has effectively lost its exclusive rights to fish in UK territorial waters, and that foreign (EU-registered) vessels are allowed to fish in UK waters, thus putting into jeopardy the sustainability of fish stocks in the North Sea in particular. An example of this from 2013 was the Dutch trawler that operates out of Hull – this vessel is said to have acquired 18% of the English fishing quota (Ungoed-Thomas, and Leake, 2013: 17). There has been an estimated 50% decline in the tonnage of fish landed by UK boats since the 1970s: some sources claimed that around 948,000 tonnes were landed in the mid – 1970s, but by 2014 this had fallen to 451,000 tonnes, and in 1984 (the year after the CFP and quotas were implemented), the UK became a net importer of fish for the first time in history. This was largely a reflection of the decline of the UK fishing fleet, which had fallen from 8,667 registered vessels in 1996 to 6,383 by 2014 (Chan, 2016e).

3.8. Other Issues

3.8.1. A European Army

The idea of a European Army (called a 'Defence Force') was first suggested by René Pleven, President of the French Council of Ministers, in a speech on 24th October, 1950. Bearing in mind that this was two years after the formation of NATO, it was a blatant attempt to wrest the defence of Europe away from that US-led defence organisation, whilst at the same time seeking to maintain the emasculation of Germany: the German Armed Forces were still not trusted, perhaps understandably so. The key, as always, was the politics behind the initiative; a European Defence Community (EDC) was a largely French idea, designed to achieve a number of political goals simultaneously: firstly, it would form a direct challenge to NATO, and as such, would be a counter-balance to the influence and involvement of the USA in Europe. Secondly, it would ensure that, through the involvement of member states, Europe would be locked into a series of mutually-supporting alliances that would ensure the safety of France, which would remain at the centre of European defence. In addition, it would have the effect of ensuring that Germany would not be able to develop as an independent military power once again. Pleven articulated the fears of many French when he said that:

"La formation de divisions allemandes, celle d'une ministère de Défence allemande, conduiraient fatelement tôt ou tard à la reconstitution d'une armée national et, par là meme, à la resurrection du militarisme allemande" (Pleven, 1950: 3).

("The formation of German divisions, of a German Ministry of defence, would sooner or later be bound to lead to the re-building of a national army and, by that token, to the revival of German militarism.")

The idea of a European Army was mentioned again by Jean Monnet, in his speech to the National Press Club, Washington DC, on 3oth April, 1952 (AEI, 1952: 1), although it is likely to have received a more lukewarm reception that when Pleven first introduced it to the French Council of Ministers. However, there was one problem – that of the role of the UK; Churchill made it clear to the House of Commons on 11th May, 1953, that whilst the UK would cooperate fully with the EDC, it would never allow its Armed Forces to be integrated into the chain of command. The future as far as the UK was concerned lay with the USA and NATO – as Churchill explained:

"We have the strongest armoured force which exists between the Elbe and the Rhine. We have very intimately associated all our air forces. We have placed our troops in Europe under the command of General Ridgeway, the NATO Commander-in-Chief....What more is there, then, that we could give, apart from completely merging ourselves with the European military organisation? We do our best for them....We shall continue to play a full and active part in plans for the political, military and economic association of Western Europe with the North Atlantic Alliance. That is, I think, a perfectly sober and reasonable statement of our position in regard to the European Defence community" (Hansard, 1953: cc 892-893).

In other words, as he said earlier in the same speech, Churchill viewed the UK military contribution as being 'with' not 'of' that of the nascent EEC. And it is this detachment that has irritated the EEC ever since: with the exception of the UK, no European country has been capable of significant military action since the early 1950s apart from France, which saw its power being diluted between the two widely-differing strategic objectives of controlling Germany, and maintaining its grip on its rapidly-deteriorating colonial empire in Africa and South-East Asia.

The fact that the UK would not commit itself to an EDC has remained an annoyance to Brussels (and the French in particular) ever since – witness the fact that the idea of a European Army has been muted on numerous occasions by just about every President of the EU, and leaders of major EU states. A European Army is something that has been muted on numerous occasions by Junker and Merkel, generally without the proposition being taken seriously as it would have been in direct conflict with NATO, and the UK could not be persuaded to join.

With the accession of the UK to the EEC in 1973, however, the situation changed, and the way to UK involvement in the development of an EDC became more likely. The extent to which the concept of an EDC or 'European Army' was still at the forefront of EU thinking was illustrated in 2015, when it was leaked to the Press that the German Chancellor (Angela Merkel) offered David Cameron help in re-negotiating the terms of UK membership of the EU, if in return he promised to back her plans for a European Army (Foster and Holehouse, 2015).

Talk of a 'Euro-Army' is worrying for NATO, which is the real defender of Europe, and which has successfully kept the Soviet Union at bay for over sixty years, yet could well be displaced by a new "Euro-Army" (Banks and Foster, 2016). The plans have been in existence for years, and in November 2016, the European Parliament voted to create what they referred to as a 'Defence Union' (Shehab, 2016), but the policy relating to the formation of a Euro-Army was only made public immediately following the UK vote to leave – the thinking behind this doubtless being that had the public become aware of what was being planned, this might have served as another reason to vote to leave the EU.

Despite the reassurances in 2000 of the then-Labour Defence Secretary, Geoff Hoon that "... the EU will not divert resources from NATO, duplicate its arrangements, create separate military structures, or conduct operational planning" (Tisdall, 2001), it would appear that the European Rapid Reaction Force (ERRF) is doing just that. As Tisdall observed:

"...General Jean-Pierre Kelche, chief of the French defence staff... reportedly insisted that the EU's proposed 60,000-strong rapid reaction force (RRF) would become operational by the end of the year with or without Nato's agreement –

and could in future conduct operations independently of the Americans and without necessarily obtaining their okay" (Tisdall, 2001).

In this he is backed by General Gustav Hagglund, Finnish Chairman of the EU's Permanent Military Committee, who has stated that the ERRF is an 'independent body', and 'not a subsidiary of NATO' (Thatcher, 2001: 43). This is exactly what NATO feared, and which the EU has repeated assured us would not happen. As for the ERRF, Margaret Thatcher suggested that, as with other EU institutions, it would eventually succumb to the fate of all multinational intervention forces – it will not be 'European' as it will be dependent on US support, nor 'Rapid', nor "...much of a force." She concluded that it will suffer from "... the old problem of all multinational intervention forces – different languages, decision by committee, divided authority, competing objectives" (Thatcher, 2001: 42). How, therefore, can the EU be trusted with our defence, especially as a defensive alliance needs strong, united political direction? This is something that the EU patently lacks: one only has to look at the EU's response to the Russian invasion and occupation of Georgia and the Ukraine for an example of the extent of confusion, procrastination and lack of unity that typifies the EU's response to major crises.

The Russian military intervention in Georgia was said to be justified by the EU as the 'breakaway' region of South Ossetia was illegal (Waterfield, 2009a) – a similar position was taken with regard to the recent troubles in Catalunya. What was not commented on at the time was the fact that the break from Georgia was fostered and supported by Russia (Mordasov, 2012). It is ironic that, some five years later, Russia tried the same tactic in their occupation of the Crimea, and the fostering of 'breakaway' groups in Eastern Ukraine. The EU was ineffectual and divided in how to respond to this illegal occupation with some countries pushing for enhanced sanctions and insisting that the Russians leave the Crimea, whilst others felt that a more softer, diplomatic approach would ultimately prove more effective (Oliver *et. al.*, 2014).

The only organisation that is currently standing up to potential Russian aggression in the Baltic States is NATO. Warnings to the Russians over their deployment of missiles in the region (Rettman, 2017), and NATO troop deployments in the Baltic (MacAskill, 2017), appear to be preventing Russia from engaging in further destabilisation and occupations. Currently, the Baltic Republics are threatened by some 766,000 Russian troops, with 15,400 tanks, 3,500 aircraft, and 350 ships; NATO forces consist of 181,500 troops, 400 tanks, around 900 aircraft and 112 ships – all of which are from Latvia, Lithuania, Estonia, and the UK, with the remainder of the EU nations contributing nothing as yet (Porter and Pouvreau, 2017:19-25). Thus, any deterrent (defence) value is a consequence of NATO military support, rather than any EU pseudo-military intervention.

Finally, and perhaps of greatest importance, is the fact that diverting expenditure from NATO to a Euro-Army might give US President Trump the excuse he needs to cut US funding for NATO – during the US election campaign of 2016, he consistently labelled NATO 'obsolete' and complained vociferously that European member states were not paying the level of contribution that they should have been doing – even though he reversed his opinion on becoming President (Kentish, 2017).

3.8.2. The Euro for All

In 2002, the respected UK Institute of Economic affairs (IEA), undertook a study of the desirability of the UK joining the Euro: the conclusion was 'no' (Minford, 2002:57). This does not appear to have reduced enthusiasm for this failed currency, famously described as a 'half-baked idea' by Sir Alan Walters when he was economic advisor to Margaret Thatcher. The obligation of all member states to eventually adopt the Euro was decided some time ago – as Rhein (2012) observes: "In the on-going debate about the future of the Euro it is often forgotten that membership in the Euro-zone is mandatory for all EU member States provided they fulfil the *Maastricht* criteria – budget deficit below 3 per cent and public debt below 60 per cent of GDP – and have achieved a satisfactory level of economic & monetary convergence (small current account imbalances and interest rates in line with Euro zone countries)."

This is recognised as necessary to the future of the Euro; in addition, some observers have also been talking about far deeper integration. In 2012, the banking crisis and subsequent crisis relating to Greece, showed that the Euro has prevented countries from devaluing – a strategy that would have prevented the worst excesses of austerity imposed by the Germans and the European Central Bank (ECB). Habermas et. al. (2012) feel that: "Only a significant consolidation of European integration can sustain a common currency without the need for a never-ending series of bailouts, which in the long term would strain the solidarity of the European national populations in the Eurozone on both sides – donor countries and recipients – to breaking point."

In this they are supported by many other politicians, economists, and EU-observers: the problem is not the logic of their argument, but the fact that they assume that all nations want deeper financial integration – a supposition which has yet to be proven. Despite this, the EU forges ahead with its plans for closer monetary union amongst those countries that use the Euro; EU financial reforms appear to be converging along the route of political control, with Brussels now pushing for the EU to have its' own representative on the board of the IMF – an idea opposed by many non-European countries (Khan, 2015:41).

Lilico (2014) claimed that membership of the Euro would be obligatory for every member state of the EU by 2020, as this was the "...stated official goal of the Italian Prime Minister, the French President, the German Chancellor, the current and next Presidents of the European Commission, the President of the European Council, and just about every significant mainstream political figure in the Eurozone."

Not surprisingly, Brussels once more chose to remain quiet; with what might be described as masterful timing, this was kept under wraps until the Brexit vote revealed that the UK was to leave the EU – after which it was presumably felt that such news could no longer influence the outcome of the referendum (O'Brien, 2016). With the vote to leave the EU, the issue is now effectively dead as far as the UK is concerned.

Chapter 4 | Immigration

4.1. Introduction

4.1.1. Immigration and 'Project Fear'

Although immigration appeared alongside others in Chapter 1.2: ("Why did the UK Vote to Leave the EU?"), it featured so strongly in people's reasons for voting 'leave', that it was decided that in order to do justice to the topic, it would require a separate chapter. From the perspective of 'Project Fear' immigration was very different to all other considerations, as it could not be used to frighten voters into backing 'remain' – the exact opposite was true, as the majority of people felt that immigration was a major issue, and one that might only be solved by leaving. For example, in a British Social Attitudes (BSA) study, published in 2016, it was revealed that, of those people surveyed, 56% wanted immigration reduced by "a lot", and 77% by "a little or a lot". This was partially explained by the fact that 36% think that on balance immigration is bad for the British economy, another 36% think that it takes jobs away from British workers, and 50% think that immigration has made crime worse (BSA, 2016: 6-7). In an interview with *The Daily Telegraph* when he was Foreign Secretary, Philip Hammond appeared to speak out against those who wanted to halt unchecked EU immigration into the UK as required by the freedom of movement aspects of EU membership: "If your ambition is that we have total unfettered control of our own borders to do what we like, that isn't compatible with membership of the European Union.... So if that's what you want, you're essentially talking about leaving the European Union" (Dominiczak, 2014b:1). It is likely that this was aimed at people who wanted to place restrictions on immigration, yet did not want to leave the EU – coming, as it did, from someone who by his own admission later voted to stay *in* the EU. The problem with emotional blackmail is that the outcome is unpredictable: there may have been those for whom immigration was such an important issue that, based on Hammond's argument, they felt that the only course of action was to vote 'leave.'

Hence, 'remainers' tended to steer clear of immigration whenever possible. Having said this, a few people and organisations tried to accentuate the benefits of immigration, but their efforts appeared to have been largely based on economics and the general benefit to the wider economy. For example, the Deputy Director at the CBI was quoted in 2015 as saying that: "Research shows that [skilled workers] have a positive impact on the UK's economy, both letting foreign firms invest and allowing companies to have international head offices here" (Warrell and Parker, 2015:3). This may well be true, but it raises one interesting issue: the implication is that neither inward investment, nor foreign company HQ locations would take place without an influx of foreign workers. By extension, she appeared to be saying that the native UK workforce was not good enough! Furthermore, how realistic was this argument when targeted at people with low levels of skills, for whom the location of international headquarters is undoubtedly a matter of supreme unimportance? They are far more concerned over immigrants who 'take' UK jobs.

4.1.2. Immigration: The Debate

Politicians have used immigration as a political 'football' for a number of years, playing on fears of job losses and/or mass migration and a loss of cultural identity. The argument both for and against economic migrants can be broadly summarised as follows: those who are in favour claim that immigration brings new skills, expertise, and low cost labour into the country, and that overall the contribution made by immigrants far outweighs any negative consequences. In contrast, those against immigration, point to the same metrics, but come to a different conclusion: they say that once aspects such as health and social services (Lawson, 2016b:20), housing (Swinford, 2015:1), and education are factored in, immigrants are a net drain on the economy, rather than being an asset.

The argument over the benefit (or otherwise) of immigration is unlikely to be solved by statistics, as people are emotional (perhaps illogically so) with regard to the issue of immigration, and are very unlikely to change their minds. This is evident when one considers the main areas that concern people, and therefore are the areas that are most likely to have motivated people to vote to 'leave' if they felt that leaving was the only way in which the UK could regain control of its borders. Certain sectors of society, perhaps with ulterior motives, have tried to label those who question unrestricted immigration as 'racists' – a charge vehemently denied, for as commentators such as O'Neill (2016) writing in *The Spectator* has pointed out "...concern about immigration isn't necessarily racism", a stance supported by many others (Pearson, 2016b:16; Hannan, 2016:18). It fell to the Conservative Cabinet Minister, Priti Patel, who is the daughter of Indian immigrants to the UK, to defend concerns with immigration. As she said in an interview with *The Daily Telegraph:* "I don't subscribe to this view that it is racist to speak about immigration and I say that as a daughter of immigrants from decades ago ...." (Hope, 2016:14-15).

4.1.3. Areas of Concern

There were (and still are) basically four areas of concern with regard to unrestricted immigration:

i) Increased Pressure on Services

Immigrants are held responsible for increased pressure (resulting in longer waiting times) for NHS services, and the fact that many parents cannot get their children into the schools they hope for, as immigrants are taking places. In 2016 the Culture Secretary (John Whittingdale) complained that high levels of immigration were putting pressure "...on all of the public services – housing, education, health. It is creaking at the seams. There is a very strong feeling that this is a small country and we simply cannot go on having an enormous influx over which we have no control" (Swinford, 2016b:13). Even Tony Blair, who as Prime Minister some thirteen years previously had encouraged the first waves of unrestricted immigration into the UK from the EU, appears to have learned the lesson of the referendum: his 'Institute for Global Change' recently published a report in which it was proposed – amongst other things - that access to healthcare should be restricted for unemployed migrants (Shipman, 2017:1). A cynical observer might well conclude that, as it has taken him thirteen years and a referendum 'defeat' to express this change of philosophy, his 'road to Damascus' moment might have more to do with reflecting the popular mood, than standing up for principles; pragmatism over principle having long been a Blair trademark.

ii) Loss of Jobs for UK Nationals

It is also claimed that immigrants will take away UK worker's jobs as immigrant labourers (especially unskilled) are generally prepared to work for less than their British counterparts – for these people, low wages may still represent higher levels of income than they could earn in their respective countries. Tellingly, since the referendum, the Labour Leader Jeremy Corbyn has stated publicly that one of the reasons his party supports leaving the EU, is because of the "... wholesale importation of underpaid workers from central Europe in order to destroy conditions, particularly in the construction industry." He also suggested that, if elected, he would ask employers to advertise jobs locally first – rather than advertise across the EU – something that is prevented under EU legislation as it is classed as discriminatory. He said that foreign workers would be allowed to come to the UK "...on the basis of the jobs available and their skill sets to go with it. What we wouldn't allow is this practice by agencies, who are quite disgraceful they way they do it – recruit a workforce, low paid – and bring them here in order to dismiss an existing workforce in the construction industry, then pay them low wages. It's appalling. And the only people who benefit are the companies" (Marr, 2017:3). All of which would suggest that Labour feels that the EU undermines the rights and job opportunities of British workers.

iii) Immigrant Access to State Support

In an interview with *The Daily Telegraph* in December 2015, the Czech secretary of State for Foreign Affairs warned Cameron that he could not make EU immigrants wait for four years before receiving in-work benefits, unless he placed the same restrictions on UK nationals at the same time (Day and Foster, 2015:19). In 2014 it was revealed that the UK government was being told to pay unemployment benefits to EU citizens who became unemployed in the UK – some of whom have since returned to their own countries: the figure being talked about was £10 million, and what was even worse, the Commission was insisting that such payments are made, regardless of the legality of any claims: "The Commission agrees decisions should be applied irrespective of whether they are legally binding or not because the workability of the whole system depends on it" (Day and Waterfield, 2014b:8). In a further twist, in April 2017 it was reported that, as part of the Brexit negotiations, the EU was pushing to make the British government pay child benefit to migrant workers in the UK, even if their dependents were living outside the UK (Barker *et. al.,* 2017:1). In other words, we have lost the ability to decide who receives state benefit, and the decision is made by the very governments that, unable to provide for their own nationals, have encouraged their people to relocate to the UK. In addition, once EU immigrants have resided in the UK for a period of three months, they are entitled to claim 'jobseekers allowance'[26], and in some cases they are able to claim housing benefit – one is forced to question exactly how it can be claimed that such people make a valuable contribution to UK society?

There is one other class of 'immigrant' into the UK that has the right to receive financial benefits – students who come here for full-time education. As EU citizens they are entitled to the same benefits as their UK counterparts, and are also entitled to receive a student loan (underwritten by the UK government) – if they have lived [note: *lived* not *worked*] in the UK for at least five years prior to their application.[27] In itself this is not a problem, as such loans are repaid when a certain earnings figure is reached by graduates, and money deducted at source by employers, to be sent to the UK Revenue & Customs. The problem is that many foreign students do not repay their loans, and pursuing them is difficult when they return to their respective countries (Perraudin and Adams, 2016). The *EUobserver* (2014) cites sources that claim up to €48 billion is owed by EU students to the UK Student Loans Company (SLC), and that "...students from Romania, Lithuania and Bulgaria take the money and return home without repayment." If this abuse is widespread, then it ultimately becomes a drain on the UK taxpayer, and as such, should be stopped immediately – unfortunately this is impossible to do, as EU citizens have the same rights as

---

26. https://www.citizensadvice.org.uk/benefits/coming-from-abroad-and-claiming-benefits-the-habitual-residence-test/eea-nationals-and-the-habitual-residence-test/eea-nationals-claiming-benefits-as-a-jobseeker/
27. https://www.gov.uk/government/news/funding-support-for-eu-students

UK citizens – for whom it is much easier to extract loan repayments from their earnings.

iv) Increase in Crime and Terrorism

Another immigrant-related factor that worries people, is the potential for an increase in general crime, which is always an important issue, but for many it is made worse by our inability to stop foreign criminals entering the UK. In 2014, for example a Romanian – convicted twice of burglary in his own country, could not be prevented from entering the UK, where he burgled and sexually assaulted an elderly woman in her home. He was subsequently convicted and jailed for 16 years. The Suffolk Police and Crime Commissioner said: "It's completely unacceptable that foreign nationals with previous custodial sentences are allowed into this country....The law needs to be changed immediately" (*Telegraph* Reporter, 2014: 8). Some months later, a Polish national who had been convicted of rape in Poland used fake ID to enter the UK where he committed the same offence again (Clarke-Billings, 2015:11).

In some of the more worrying examples of immigration, it was revealed that certain nations were selling residency visas and passports: Hungary, for example, was said to be offering "...residency visas for people who make a €250,000 investment in government bonds" (Wise, 2014:1). A *Daily Telegraph* investigation in 2014 revealed that to get a Bulgarian passport, all that was needed was to spend two days in the country and pay a fee to a broker of £150,000 (Watt *et. al,* 2014: 1/6). The fear is that if immigrants are accepted by any EU nation, and acquire citizenship (and passport), then as long as the UK remains a member of the EU, such people cannot be prevented from coming to the UK. Added to these concerns were (and still are) the growing worries over terrorism, and the fact that much of Europe is currently being targeted by Muslim terrorists, many of whom have European passports – which means that they cannot be prevented from coming into the UK. Attitudes have hardened further since their admission, in February 2016, that the German authorities had'lost track' of 130,000 asylum seekers, especially as some appeared to have disappeared using false passports, which were believed to come from "...the same source as those used by some of the Paris attackers" (Huggler, 2016:9).

An Editorial in *The Daily Telegraph* pointed out that the leaders of Germany "...are slowly coming to terms with the fact that some migrants, or even refugees, can be criminal – and that some cultures do not relocate easily to Western soil" (Editorial, 2016a:21). The obvious worry is that if these people have EU passports, they have access to unrestricted travel within those countries that are members of the Schengen agreement, and the potential to cross national frontiers unrecorded – the person responsible for the attack on the 2016 Berlin Christmas market, was thought to have travelled through three countries without a problem, before being caught in Italy. Similarly, the French Syrian who murdered four visitors to the Jewish Museum in Brussels crossed easily from Frankfurt to France. A European counter-terrorism chief, who wished to remain anonymous, complained that Schengen "…is the number one concern – the big problem that we are struggling with…. To try to find a way to properly track all of these foreign fighters is already very hard. The lack of information because of Schengen makes it nearly impossible" (Jones and Robinson, 2014:7). Once security forces have lost track of these people, they can attempt to get into the UK – generally under the guise of 'asylum seekers' – as such people generally enter the country without documentation, it is difficult to assess their backgrounds. A former Head of Counter-terrorism at the Metropolitan Police was quoted as saying: "Schengen poses a huge risk of terrorism. Porous borders across mainland Europe are continuing to be exploited by Isil" (Swinford *et. al,* 2016:1). This was confirmed when it was found that of the nine attackers who killed 130 people at the Bataclan theatre in Paris in November 2015, seven had passed through a numbers of European countries, posing as refugees (Pancevski, 2016:22).

4.1.4. The EU Dictates Immigrant Numbers

In a policy statement that must have presented 'remainers' with a veritable headache, the EU decided to increase the number of immigrants without visa to the EU. The European Commission proposed reforms to EU asylum rules that would see stiff financial penalties imposed on countries refusing to take their 'share' of asylum seekers (Hall and Holehouse, 2015:18): later commentators suggested that the EU was contemplating 'fining' member states up to £200,000 for each person that they do not accept as a refugee (BBC, 2016b). The Austrians are particularly aggrieved at having to bear the brunt of the refugee influx, and the Austrian Interior minister warned that unless other EU states took more refugees there was a growing possibility that Europe would 'fail' as a consequence of what she regarded as an unfair burden on the Austrian people (Alexander *et.al.,* 2015:12-13).

The message over quotas has not gone down well in Poland, Hungary, Slovakia, and the Czech Republic, all of which broadly oppose the imposition of quotas: these countries, known collectively as the Visegrad Group, all oppose the obligatory quota system outlined by the EU, instigated by the Germans (who have tacitly admitted that Merkel's policy of 'open door' asylum was a mistake), and railroaded through in a matter of weeks by Juncker in yet another attempt to reduce opposition to EU diktat. The rationale being that if so-called 'asylum seekers' are spread throughout Europe, then their impact will not be as noticeable as if they were concentrated in one or two zones, thus alienating the native population, and leading to resentment against Brussels. An unnamed senior diplomat from Eastern Europe is quoted as having said: "You are not going to resolve this very serious issue in three weeks with procedures that are rushed through in panic mode....Juncker is saying he does not really care what the leaders think" (Robinson and Foy, 2015:5).

In September 2015, Poland's Foreign Minister said: "Each country must be able to decide how many migrants it can receive" (Nolan *et. al.,* 2015: 18). Indeed, in Hungary, Prime Minister Victor Orban has consistently opposed this edict saying, in 2016 that "Every single migrant poses a public security and terror risk" (Byrne, 2016:6), and according to the latest referendum (October 2016), his stance is supported by some 98% of voters (Barker and Byrne, 2017: 6).

The prospect of yet more migrants entering the country as part of an obligatory quota, must surely have been reason enough for many people in the UK to vote 'leave' as the only way of stopping this in future. By June 2013, net migration to the UK had risen by 182,000 (9%), largely fuelled a 25,000 increase in migration from the EU, making it impossible to achieve the government's target of cutting the net flow of immigration by 2015 (Warrell, 2013:6). Even David Cameron appeared to acknowledge that immigration had reached uncontrollable proportions when he admitted in 2013 that immigration into the UK "… had been 'too fast' and 'too high in recent years…" and that he was determined to "… prevent people from abusing our benefits system…" (Hannah Kuchler and Rigby, 2013:5). This was Cameron reacting to the growing undercurrent of popular opinion, which was broadly anti-immigration, and which was expressed some five months later in a YouGov poll of voting intentions prior to the Euro elections of 2014; this placed UKIP and the Conservatives neck-and-neck, on 29% and 28% respectively.

The importance of this indicator for the Conservatives was that the same poll found that 35% of those question said that UKIP had the best policies on immigration – as opposed to 17% for the Conservatives (Shipman, 2014:19). This suggested that to beat UKIP, the Conservatives would have to bow to the wishes of the electorate, and endorse a stronger anti-immigration policy. As previously explained, the then Foreign Secretary, Philip Hammond, tried emotional blackmail over immigration to persuade people to vote remain (Dominiczak, 2014b:1): neither he nor Cameron obviously appreciated the strength of public opinion on this issue. David Cameron, could not get Brussels to agree to restrictions on migration, and instead tried to tackle the problem by appealing to UK industry to invest more in training the native population to fill employment 'gaps,' rather than relying on overseas workers (Warrell, and Parker, 2015:3). The government failed to account for the number of immigrants, and by March 2016 (three months before the referendum) official figures showed that 257,000 EU migrants came to live in the UK in 2014.

4.2. The Cultural Legacy of Mass Immigration

In addition to the effects of immigration already mentioned, there is arguably a far greater problem: that of the cultural implications of mass migration, which is slowly changing the accepted cultural norms of the country. It is this latter factor, perhaps more than any other that worries many UK citizens. One of the most outspoken critics of the way in which immigration is changing the fabric of UK society is the MEP Nigel Farage, who noted that it is the 'ordinary' families that are paying the price for mass immigration, and it (immigration) had done "...great damage to the cohesion of our society and the well-being of working people in this country." In a speech to the 2014 UKIP conference, he asked:

"But what about the social price of this? The fact that in scores of our cities and market towns, this country in a short space of time has frankly become unrecognisable. Whether it is the impact on local schools and hospitals, whether it is the fact that in many parts of England you don't hear English spoken any more. This is not the kind of community we want to leave to our grandchildren" (Hope, 2014:6)

Worries over immigration are not just confined to the UK: increasingly even those East European states that are net financial beneficiaries from membership are becoming concerned by the 'free movement of labour' policy which is now " ...forcing them to take in thousands of migrants they do not want from across Africa and the Middle East" (Murray, 2015). In Germany, a country that had previously welcomed migrants, there is a growing backlash, with the German Federal Office for Migration and Refugees reporting a significant fall in refugee numbers in 2016, and the Federal Ministry of Finance budgeting £37 billion for refugees in the financial year 2016-2017 (McFadyen, 2017). It is little wonder that the German population is showing increasingly little appetite for the EU policies relating to the acceptance and re-settlement of refugees, and attitudes towards migrants are hardening: witness the statistics released by the German Federal Ministry of the Interior which showed that for 2016 there was an increase in migrants returning to their country of origin – 55,000 returned home voluntarily, and around 25,000 were forcibly deported by the authorities (Hill, 2017).

In Germany, news of the sexual assaults on women by migrants over the Christmas 2015 period eventually leaked out (despite the German Authorities' attempts to keep the scandal quiet) and understandably contributed to the reversal of German attitudes to these people (Noak, 2016). In January 2016, the Prime Minister of Slovakia Robert Fico, called for a summit of EU leaders "...to discuss fresh reports of migrant-led sex attacks emerging from Germany, Switzerland, Sweden, Austria and Finland..." (Foster *et. al.*, 2016:1). Despite all the evidence to the contrary, including statements of victims, witnesses, and the police, the EU refused to acknowledge a link between immigration and these appalling attacks: Frans Timmermans, Juncker's Deputy is alleged to have commented that the crimes in Cologne were a 'matter of public order' and 'not related to the refugee crisis.'

A report in *The Economist* (2016f:32-33) detailed how groups in Belgium and Norway are trying to educate male immigrants how to interact with females: "... Belgium plans to make sex education mandatory for all asylum seekers by next year [2017], as it already is in Norway. In Germany, too, the government decided in July to shift the focus of its integration courses from language learning to cultural values, including equality of the sexes."

The response to such initiatives has been at best lukewarm, at worst hostile – after all, not only do countries have to feed, clothe, and educate refugees, but now it appears that they also having to provide courses on moral values for these people, in the hope that it will prevent more sexual assaults. No wonder that Robert Fico said "The idea of a multicultural Europe has failed..." and he told the EU that Slovakia would accept no refugees as they were "...impossible to integrate..." and had a "...different relationship to women" (Holehouse, 2016a:6).

4.3. Illegal Immigration

Under the Dublin Regulation, asylum seekers must seek permanent refuge in the first EU country they enter, and cannot claim refuge anywhere else. As the majority of migrants coming from the Middle East and Africa are likely to enter the EU via Greece, Italy, and Spain, this should be where they remain. The reality is that prior to Chancellor Merkel opening the borders to such people, those that made their way through France in an attempt to get to the UK were committing an offence, and should have been detained by the French authorities – which, of course did not happen, as the French were (and still are) happy to push the problem across the English Channel. It is a highly-sensitive issue, and is perhaps most keenly felt with regard to the estimated 5,000 so-called migrants camped around Calais, waiting for the chance to illegally enter the UK (Dowling, 2015:6).

This squatter camp is known as 'The Jungle', and has been the focus for rising levels of violence directed at both private and commercial traffic trying to use the Channel Tunnel (Chazan and Rothwell, 2016; Gutteridge, 2016a). The UK border controls established on French soil are a consequence of a bilateral agreement between the UK and French governments, signed at the *Treaty of Le Touquet* in 1993, and ratified in 2000. As such, they are completely unrelated to membership of the EU: however, this did not stop people such as the new French President Emmanuel Macron (then Economy Minister) claiming that in the event of a Brexit vote, the Calais camp would 'move to Dover' as the French would "... refuse to police the section of the British border located by the Calais port and tunnels" (Speed, 2016).

Needless to say, since his elevation to the Presidency of France, Macron has been remarkably quiet over such drastic measures. His current 'Gallic charm' offensive is designed to make the UK pay more for these border controls – and Theresa May has reportedly agreed to a £44 million payment to the French authorities to help increase security in and around the port and Channel Tunnel at Calais (Rayner *et. al.* 2018:1), despite the fact that it is the responsibility of the French to ensure that their borders are properly policed. The illegals continued to cause problems in and around Calais – stopping lorries, placing burning tyres in the road, and harassing motorists, and this disruption went on for over a year (Samuel, 2014:13 and 2015:13), in addition to significant rises in crime (including gun crime) as smugglings gangs fought amongst themselves (Samuel, 2016:7). Aside from the danger to life and limb caused by these criminals, there is also the disruption to trade caused by their activities: during the summer of 2015, business could not export or import, in some cases losing thousands of pounds a day (Loizou *et. al.*, 2015:2) – major road links to the channel ports were blocked on the French side by gangs of criminals, and on the English side through miles of parked lorries that could make no progress (Rayner, 2015b:4); all David Cameron could do was to warn people that the disruption was likely to continue, saying: "This is going to be a difficult issue right across the summer" (Rayner, 2015a:4). Since then the situation has become worse, with thousands of illegal immigrants trying to get into the UK (Barrett, 2015). Eventually, even the French were shamed into taking action, and in October 2016 the authorities moved in to dismantle the camp.

Whilst it is undoubtedly true that voters 'lump together' illegal immigrants with those who have entered the country legally, it is equally true that both are popularly classified as a 'drain' on resources – illegal immigrants possibly less so, as they cannot apply for state aid. It cannot, however, have helped the case for 'remain' that in August 2015, the UK was treated to the sight of hundreds of illegals trying to get across the channel by stowing away on lorries, and in some cases, even walking though the channel tunnel (Pugh, 2015). In one week in July 2015, British police caught eighty illegals who had made it into the UK by train (Dowling, 2015:6), and it is likely that this was just the tip of the iceberg. The latest figures showed that legal net migration had reached an all-time high of 330,000, of which 269,000 were from EU countries (Warrell and Parker, 2015:3).

In a survey of March 2016, just three months before the referendum, 55% of those polled said that 'immigration' was the most important issue facing the UK; second was the NHS (52%), and third British membership of/relationship with the EU. When asked which issues would influence the way they intended to vote, it was perhaps unsurprising that 49% said 'immigration', 'How the EU is Run/who runs the EU' (36%), and 31% said the state of the UK economy (Mann, 2016). The evidence suggests that immigration (legal or otherwise) was the singlemost important reason why people voted to leave.

In 2015, The German state of Bavaria threatened to turn back asylum seekers from entering Germany via the southern route; even in the most 'migrant-friendly' country in the EU, resentment against mass immigration had reached breaking point, as shown in a poll carried out by the television station ZDF, which found that 51% of those questioned believed that Germany could not cope with the high numbers arriving, which Horst Seehofer, the Bavarian prime minister (and a political ally of Chancellor Merkel) described her immigration policy as "...a mistake we will be dealing with for a long time" (Huggler, 2015:6). By October 2015, Merkel was struggling to justify her policy to an increasingly sceptic German population, with opposition coming from those who were regarded as 'pro' immigration: the former human rights activist Joachim Gauk is reported as having said: "Our reception capacity is limited" (Pancevski, 2015:32). Only after intense pressure from political colleagues such as Wolfgang Schäuble (the German Finance Minister) has Merkel moved to attend to the German's refuge/migrant problem: she has restricted cash benefits for refugees, and has added three more countries – Albania, Kosovo, and Montenegro – to the list of countries to which it is safe to return migrants (Wagstyl, 2015:6).

Brexit: KBO

Chapter 5 | Brexit Contagion

5.1. Introduction

From the point of view of the EU stalwarts, apart from the economic consequences to the remaining members of the EU club of the UK's departure, there is a potential consequence that is far worse – 'Brexit Contagion'. Key figures in the EU were worried from the outset that even holding a referendum (let alone achieving a 'leave' vote) might prove attractive for other countries – foremost amongst which is Greece (FT Reporters, 2015:4). Four months before the UK referendum, Tusk confessed that he was 'really afraid' that the UK's referendum would prove to be "...a very attractive model for some politicians in Europe to achieve some internal, very egotistical goals" (Milne and Spiegel, 2016:11) – presumably he had politicians such as Marine Le Pen in mind. How ironic that a senior EU politician had the temerity to accuse nationally-elected politicians of 'egotism', when the unaccountable EU Commission largely functions as an extension of the egotistical desire of the President of the Commission.

Furthermore, if as Juncker claims, all other countries are highly supportive of the EU, then why not let countries hold referenda on whether to leave or remain? The only way to be certain of a nation's loyalty to the EU would be to give each member state the option of a referendum on continued membership, possibly once every decade; however, this will never happen, as to do so would highlight the palpable tide of discontent throughout much of Europe, and would bring an inherent instability into what is already an organisation that is rapidly crumbling from within.

Writing in *The Spectator* in October 2015 (when it was thought that the UK referendum would be held in 2017), Douglas Murray pointed out that "...even if the UK votes to stay in the EU in 2017, we might be one of the only countries left. It's a radical thought, but if they'd like to consider it, the Europhiles should look at what is happening across the continent" (Murray, 2015). He went on to detail the various 'Eurosceptic' parties throughout Europe, beginning with the Netherlands in which a 2015 poll showed that "... 83 per cent of Dutch voters want 'more influence' over future transfers of power to the EU and 61 per cent of the population want a referendum on any further enlargement of the EU." More recently, Bickerton (2018:16) has pointed out that "Brexit should not be treated as a stand-alone phenomenon, isolated from the rest of the continent." The extent to which Brexit may indeed 'contaminate' of EU members is highly uncertain; what is not uncertain, however, is that 'contamination' is a distinct possibility – and one that is increasingly likely if the EU refuses to reform.

Since the announcement of Brexit, the EU has sought to turn the situation to its advantage by trying to ensure that those who leave suffer heavily. As the ex-President of France (François Hollande) said: "It can serve as a lesson for those who seek the end of Europe….Populists have to know the consequences, so that the people can make up their mind" (Chassany and Barker, 2016:5). This shows a bullying, vindictive attitude on the part of at least one national leader (and his view is likely to be echoed by the other partner in the Franco-German alliance). It is a disgraceful way to behave, effectively telling countries that if they try to leave the EU, they will suffer the same fate as the UK, giving lie to the image of the EU as a group of equals, whose sole objective was the well-being of the citizens of Europe. As Janet Daley asked rhetorically: "What kind of organization threatens people who want to leave? Offhand, I can think of only three examples: mafia families, secret societies attempting to undermine the existing order, and religious cults. Arguably the European Union is a bit of all those, contrary to its view of itself as the very model of an idealistic, enlightened political entity" (Daley, 2018:20).

5.2. Opposition to the EU

5.2.1. UK Opposition

It is irrefutable that the most Eurosceptic member state has always been the UK, where the 'EU-nisation' of Europe has generally been viewed with suspicion: the British tend to equate such initiatives with central control, and a loss of individualism and hard-won historical freedoms. The British are criticised for their lack of commitment to such 'Euro-projects', and for their unwillingness to share sovereignty with other nations. There is much truth in this accusation, and with good reason. To understand the rationale behind this point of view, one only has to consider the two world wars that devastated the continent in 1914-18, and 1939-45, and the Napoleonic Wars of a century earlier. Those who criticise the British for their reticence at plunging wholeheartedly into the EU experiment forget that, on at least these three separate occasions, it has been the UK's detachment from continental institutions that has enabled the country to remain a base for operations to liberate the continent from occupation by a foreign power – generally Germany or France.

Despite (or possibly because of) the debt owed by the peoples of continental Europe to the UK, the level of resentment at British actions and attitudes is palpable. How ironic, therefore, that the French (who could not liberate themselves from German occupation in WW1 or WW2), should have had to rely on the Americans, British, and Canadians for liberation from occupation, and post – WW2 economic success and the defence of Europe. The relationship that the French have with the British is emotional: they realise that they owe the UK (amongst others) a debt of liberation, yet it is intensely painful to admit it. This is understandable, as a nation that cannot control its own destiny is surely not a nation. Therein lies the reason why the French under President De Gaulle opposed UK membership of the EEC – to bring an ancient protagonist (and one to whom France is indebted for their liberation during both world wars) into a union of supposed equals is, at very least, uncomfortable. De Gaulle also wished to limit British influence in Continental institutions, arguably because Britain might assume de facto leadership – a role that he considered to be the prerogative of the French.

Opposition to (and concerns about) the EU in its many manifestations is not something that has suddenly emerged, but began even before the act of UK Accession was signed, with a growing undercurrent of criticism and an apparent level of confusion over issues such as the reduction of tariffs for member states of the EEC – suggesting that the Customs Union (the exemplar of Free Trade) had not been properly considered by the Labour government of Harold Wilson. When The Secretary of State for Foreign and Commonwealth Affairs (Mr. Michael Stewart) was asked about this in the House of Commons on 17 March 1969, he replied: "There is not necessarily anything incompatible between our desire to enter the European Economic Community and bilateral reductions but, as has been explained in the House, any proposal of this kind would from our point of view need to be clearly linked with our entry into the Community" (*Hansard*, 1969: 19). He did not, however, elaborate further on this linkage.

Ironically, in view of the consternation and division that the UK application was apparently causing amongst existing EEC members, Mr Neil Marten (Conservative) asked whether the Foreign Secretary was "...aware that some of us on this side of the House are genuinely concerned to see the unity of the Continent of Europe and many of us believe that our continued application to join the Common Market is, rightly or wrongly, a divisive force...? Is it not, therefore, time we were a little less selfish and withdrew our application for the time being? (Hansard, 1969: 20).

In February 1970, the government published a White Paper on UK entry to the Common Market – "*Britain and the European Communities (White Paper)*" – in which the basic terms of membership were set out, and this was debated in the House of Commons on 24th and 25th February 1970, highlighting a series of genuine concerns amongst politicians. Mr Michael Stewart MP was defending the Labour Government's position against a barrage of doubt and uncertainty not only from the Opposition benches, but also from his own side. As Conservative MP Sir Harmar Nicholls pointed out, there was widespread concern over the effects of EEC membership on UK trade – in particular with Commonwealth countries: "When we sign the *Treaty of Rome* it means that we have to end trading relations with other parts of the world, particularly the Commonwealth, which would more than outweigh what we are likely to gain from entry" (Hansard, 1970a: 1008). Stewart dodged the issue, by referencing a series of confusing statistics from recent surveys showing differences of opinion over the potential benefits of membership. From the Labour benches, Mr Douglas Jay MP, suggested that "...if the right hon. Gentleman's argument now is that it is quite impossible to calculate the consequences of entering the E.E.C., would it not be better to withdraw the application until we know what the consequences would be? (Hansard, 1970a: 1022).

Others, with apparent prescience in view of what has happened (in particular since the signing of the Maastricht Treaty) were worried about the longer-term implications of the UK being forced into becoming part of a Federal Europe. Mr. Raphael Tuck MP (Labour), pointed out that, on joining the EEC eventually:

"...we would have to go into a federal union. The Treaty of Rome implies it even though it does not mention it in terms. Our parliamentary democracy would disappear and we would be subordinate to the Six. The laws passed by the Commission would apply to us and it is estimated that 2,000 of our own laws and regulations would have to be changed. My right hon. Friend the Foreign Secretary, although he has no authority for it, is a member of the Monnet Committee for the United States of Europe. We have to ask ourselves this question: do we wish to retain democracy as we know it, or do we throw it to the winds for a nebulous advantage which is not plain to anyone, not even Her Majesty's Government? I remind the House that, if we go in, we shall not be in a situation like that of N.A.T.O., which we can leave. This would be permanent. There would be no getting out" (Hansard, 1970a: Vol. 796, c.1116).

Mr Robin Turton MP (Conservative) was another member of Parliament who articulated the concerns of the public, claiming that "...72 per cent. of the British people are opposed to Britain going into the Common Market." He went on to point out that the British people:

"... do not want to be subject to an authoritarian bureaucracy, and they believe that that would be the answer if we went into the Community. The British people also feel unhappy about the political stability of the members of the Six, and they do not want to be in a United States of Europe with them.... I think that the majority of the British people feel that they would not wish to betray the Australians, New Zealanders and Canadians or abandon their partners in E.F.T.A. in exchange for some federal solution with a United States of Europe.... Last night, the hon. Member for Watford (Mr. Raphael Tuck) quoted Dr. Luns, the Dutch Foreign Minister, who said, when he came over here, that Britain would be accepted only if she agreed to have a federal solution with the Six. I hope that the Prime Minister will explain exactly what we would be entering if these negotiations succeeded" (Hansard, 1970b:1249).

There were many other fears expressed by MPs, too many to include in this short book; the point is that even before the UK's entry into the EEC, there was disquiet at what membership would mean for the country, especially in terms of trade and the UKs sovereignty – two issues that remained key in the 2016 referendum. In addition to issues relating to corruption, nepotism, and waste of resources (Craig and Elliott, 2009), by the late 1980s there was the looming question of German re-unification: many were afraid that this would upset the balance of power both within Europe and the EEC. Sir William Cash, had warned both Margaret Thatcher and John Major of 'creeping Federalism' in the EU, as this was particularly apparent in the new Maastricht Treaty, which Major would have to sign in his capacity as UK Prime Minister; Cash wrote:

"…on February 7, 1992, John Major asked me what I would do if I were in his situation. 'You will have to veto the Treaty,' I said. 'Why?' asked Major. I replied: 'It will be a German Europe. Just look at what's going on in relation to interest rates and who is setting them.' 'Well if that's the case,' Major said, 'I will have to enter into an alliance with the French.' The conversation went no further — nor did any alliance with the French" (Cash, 2016).

Cash subsequently led the Conservative rebellion against the signing of the *Maastricht Treaty*. As he explained:

"The Maastricht Rebellion of the early 1990s, which I led, was the first concerted rebellion against the increasing acceleration of undemocratic European government, accompanied by political union at the expense of our national sovereignty. I put down about 150 amendments in my own name to the Treaty and set up the Maastricht Referendum Campaign and the 17 Great College Street Group in 1993. The 17 Great College Street Group conducted its operations from 17 Great College Street itself with an extensive staff of researchers and activists in preparing briefing papers for the 150 amendments" (Private correspondence with author, 27th March, 2018).

Opposing one's own government is never something that an MP undertakes lightly, but as Cash explained:

"The reason for the Referendum campaign was that I recognised that the collusion between the two front benches, Labour and Conservative, meant that there would never be a parliamentary majority to prevent our being further drawn into the process of EU political integration with or without the euro. The increase in majority voting would make the UK parliament (under Sections 2 and 3 of the European Communities Act and the increasing volume of EU competences) increasingly subservient to the EU with consequent impotence and subservience as our sovereignty was whittled away. This rebellion, which is well documented, continued until eventually even the Conservative Party voted against the Lisbon Treaty but then failed to deliver a Referendum under David Cameron. This was remedied by the amendment against a 3-line whip which I drafted (put forward by David Nuttall) which achieved a critical mass of 81 Conservative back benchers. This broke the camel's back and then a series of Referendum private members bills ultimately led to the Bloomberg Speech and the eventual passing of the Referendum Act itself in 2015" (Private correspondence with author, 27th March, 2018).

Thus, the whole issue of a referendum on membership was a consequence of growing dissatisfaction and resentment amongst disparate sectors of society, and the irony is that the majority of those who were dissatisfied would have been happy with a reformed EU, rather than having to leave it altogether. However, as will become obvious, the intransigence and arrogance of EU leaders meant that they would not make concessions – in the end, therefore, the UK was forced into a simple binary decision: 'leave' or 'remain.'

Notwithstanding half a century of peace in Europe, Stephens observes that: "The British, or more properly, the English, will never love the European Union. The relationship is one of realism rather than emotional attachment" (Stephens, 2011). Occasionally such feelings are made public, and in view of the fragility of the EU-UK relationships, have to be stifled. In July 1990, for example, the UK Cabinet Minister Nicholas Ridley criticised the lack of accountability in the EU hierarchy. This was by no means an unusual outburst, but what was different, was the frame of reference for the attack:

"When I look at the institutions to which it is proposed that sovereignty is to be handed over, I'm aghast…unelected reject politicians with no accountability to anybody, who are not responsible for raising taxes, just spending money, who are pandered to by a supine parliament which is also not responsible for raising taxes, already behaving with an arrogance I find breathtaking; the idea that one says 'OK, so we'll give this lot our sovereignty' is unacceptable to me. I'm not against giving up sovereignty in principle, but not to this lot. You might as well give it to Adolf Hitler, frankly" (Ridley, 1990).

Whilst the sentiments Ridley expressed were understood (and probably largely agreed with), his 'crime' was to have compared the EU to the Nazis. Ridley suggested that Helmut Kohl (then German leader) would "…soon be coming here and telling us that this is what we should do on the banking front and this is what our taxes should be" (Ridley, 1990) – which, of course, is almost exactly what Angela Merkel did with the Greeks some twenty-five years later. Ridley was sacked for his comments, although some years later, Dominic Lawson suggested that Ridley should have been congratulated for his perception (Lawson, 2011). The situation was (unintentionally) exacerbated by EU officials, who, by 2012, were labelling Berlin the 'capital' of Europe, and suggesting that: "France needs Germany to disguise how weak it is. Germany needs France to disguise how strong it is…" (Rachman, 2012a).

5.2.2. EU Opposition

A major reason behind the intervention by leading politico-economic figures is the fear that a British exit will open the door to other nations contemplating leaving, and that their influence will be reduced as a consequence. Juncker, when asked whether Brexit would mean the break-up of the EU answered emphatically 'no.' He is out of touch with the reality of the situation, as most major European countries have anti-EU parties, all of which wish to leave the EU, and are campaigning for just such an outcome. As was apparent in the recent French Presidential elections, these nationalist parties are increasingly appealing to disenfranchised voters, and if they become politically influential, it could mean the break-up of the EU, which is something that is viewed with horror by those organisations that regard the EU as providing a stable platform for high – powered (and well-paid) jobs, and global politico-economic influence. In 2009, the EU Parliament commissioned a survey to assess their level of support amongst the voters; that they should even have considered doing this is telling, as it suggested that the Parliament (the only truly elected body in the EU), was worried about a lack of popularity. Overall support was found to have declined considerably: in France, for example, only 47% of those surveyed were positive about the country's membership of EU, as compared with 74% in 1987 (Hall, 2009).

There may be a relationship between this growing dislike of the EU and the French attitude to regulations from Brussels: an EU report assessed attitudes towards EU legislation between 1997 and 2000, and found that France was the worst offender for infringements of internal market regulations; the Commission investigated a total of 224 incidents compared with 192 incidents for Italy, and 76 for the UK. Even the French press was scathing, with *La Tribune* saying that: "The French are Europeans when it suits them. France has once again lived up to its reputation as a prickly partner ready to claim exceptional circumstances when its own interests clash with those of the community" (Willsher, 2002:5).

The last time EU citizens had been asked their opinion of the EU was in *The Eurobarometer Survey* (2013). This found a decline of 26% in the number of respondents who said that they 'trust' the EU (Chaffin, 2013). Of particular interest is the emergence of a strong Eurosceptic group in Finland – a country that was traditionally regarded as a key supporter of the EU (Dinmore, 2013).

In many respects, anti-EU parties are similar to the United Kingdom Independence Party (UKIP), and if they garner sufficient support may well force their respective governments to hold a referendum on membership – exactly as happened in the UK. As Carter (2016) observed:

"The fact that currently one-third of MEPs represent Eurosceptic parties is indicative of a problem that cannot be ignored, practically or ethically. The low turn-outs at European Parliament elections, just 42.6 per cent on average in 2014, are reason enough to take Eurosceptisim seriously.... The EU must respond by listening to its citizens and responding to their concerns, particularly on the repatriation of powers from Brussels. This is something which, according to a recent report by Statstica, 42 per cent of Europeans want to see, versus only 19 per cent who favour further supranational centralisation of power. To limit Brexit contagion, and to create an organisation representative of its citizens, the EU must listen..."

But who are these Eurosceptic parties, and what percentage of their respective populations do they represent? In France the high profile Marine Le Pen (of the Front National (FN)) recently lost the Presidential election to Emmanuel Macron, but still gained 34% of the national vote (Christafis, 2017) – this was an historically high level for the FN, and one that shows that around one third of the French electorate who voted considered the FN as the best political party to represent their outlook. The FN is anti-immigration, anti-Euro, and anti-EU, preferring to repatriate most decision-making powers back to France.

Ironically for a French political party, it has been given a new impetus by the UK Brexit vote; the *FT* quoted a typical French supporter of the FN, who thought that the British were 'simply brilliant' for their decision to leave the EU: "They have had the courage to put two fingers up to Brussels... and I don't praise the British lightly" (Thomson and Stothard, 2016:9). Writing before the results of the last French Presidential election, Carter (2016) commented that: "A recent Pew Research Centre survey indicated that 61 per cent of French people view the EU negatively, suggesting a strong appetite for a referendum. Whether Le Pen wins next year or not, the NF pose a formidable threat to France's future in the European Union and social cohesion more broadly."

Other similarly-minded parties include the Finnish "True Finns", led by Timo Soini, the Dutch "Party for Freedom" (Geert Wilders), the Danish "People's Party"

(Kristian Thulesen Dahl), and the Italian "Five Star Movement" (Beppe Grillo) and the Northern League (Mateo Salvini), which is increasingly positioning itself as a national (as opposed to a regional) anti-immigration party – in direct conflict with Brussels over this issue (Politi, 2017:7).

This is by no means a complete list, but focuses on the anti-EU movements in the key countries of the EU. All pose a potential threat to the ruling elite of the EU, and have the potential to deliver another 'Brexit' at any time, providing, of course, that the EU bureaucracy and their respective governments permit an appropriate plebiscite. Even within the major powers of the EU, there is growing opposition: in Germany, for example, the AFD ("Alternative for Germany") party has registered very high levels of support – based, it is suspected, on attracting those people who feel threatened by Merkel's 'open door' policy to refugees.

5.3. Anti-Democratic Voices

Many 'remainers' have suggested that the people of the UK should not accept the referendum result, and some have even said that a second referendum should be held. This is an appalling example of people who do not accept the result of a democratically arrived-at decision. Amongst the 'wreckers' are people such as Peter Mandelson, who feels he has the right (as a member of the House of Lords) to attempt to frustrate the Brexit Bill as it goes through various stages of scrutiny; as he ultimately hopes to keep the UK in the EU (despite the wishes of the electorate), it is interesting to speculate as to the extent to which his stance is motivated by considerations for the future well-being of the UK, as opposed to the £35,000 annual pension he receives as a former EU Trade Commissioner (Swinford, 2017b:4).

If people such as Mandleson were to frustrate Brexit, halt or even reverse the process, it would be disastrous for those who believe in delivering the outcome of a democratic decision – so the danger could not be clearer. Some have framed their disdain with reference to the objections based on the democratic process: for example, Bogdanor (2017) quotes the Cabinet Secretary, Lord Butler, as inquiring why those "...who base arguments for Brexit on the will of the people are now opposed to consulting the people on the outcome of the negotiations..." To begin with, he omits to mention that 'consulting the people on the outcome of the negotiations' was never done when we were first taken into the then EEC; furthermore, it is difficult to take lectures on democracy seriously when the person speaking pontificates from his seat in the (unelected) House of Lords.

Mandelson threatened to defeat the government when they debated the Brexit Bill, or to block the legislation (Harris, 2017) as it went through the unelected debating club that passes for our second chamber. His opposition to Brexit is perhaps understandable, as for a time (2004-2008) he was the EU Trade

Commissioner, and when he resigned to take up a Cabinet position in Gordon Brown's government, he was reportedly entitled to some £1 million in EU pay offs and pension (Kirkup, 2008): surely a good example of individuals having personally benefited from their involvement with the EU? Another Lord to suggest they would vote against the Government was Michael Hesseltine (Watts, 2017), which is not surprising, as he has a history of opposing Conservative Prime Ministers; he resigned as Defence Secretary when Margaret Thatcher would not agree with him over the fate of Westland Helicopters, and he later challenged her for the Leadership of the Party. Apart from his disloyalty to the then PM, Hesseltine is probably most famous for throwing the House of Commons' Mace onto the floor in a fit of temper.

The Liberal Democrat Lord Paddick argued that "...the British people did not know the full consequences of leaving the EU at the time of the referendum and they did not therefore make an informed choice" (Stone, 2017). This is indeed true, but as argued at the start of this book, neither side ('leave' or 'remain') could adequately back up their case with facts – instead we were treated to speculation and 'Project Fear' so Paddick is perhaps being somewhat disingenuous. Furthermore, when the various EU treaties were signed that gave away the UK's sovereignty and independence piece by piece (see chapter 3.2 "EU Expansion"), the UK public were not even given a vote, and the matter of ever – closer integration was presented to them by a largely-acquiescent House of Commons, and 'nodded through' (in more ways than one) by the House of Lords. Baron Hain (a Cabinet Minister under Tony Blair) claimed that "...despite being an unelected peer he has the right to force major changes to the Brexit Bill..." (Swinford, 2017a: 4). Comments such as these are illustrative of people totally divorced from the realties and pressures of current politico-financial realities, and who feel that because of their privileged position, they have the right to dictate and lecture to the rest of the population. They do not. People who find themselves on the losing side in a popular vote cannot call for a re-run simply because they are unhappy with the result.

To suggest that the public were not fully aware of all the issues surrounding Brexit is both true and at the same time mischievous, as the public are never aware of all the issues in any general election – yet the result of such exercises in democracy are respected by all concerned. It should be pointed out that even when political intentions are telegraphed with sufficient clarity and far enough in advance of the date on which a national decision is to be made (for example, in a General Election Manifesto), the electorate can still never be certain that promises will be adhered to if the party making the promises were to win power.

There are two recent examples of this, the most recent being the apparent promise made by Jeremy Corbyn that if Labour were elected to government, he would reduce (some claimed he said he would 'scrap') tuition fees for university students. He gave an interview to the *New Musical Express* – a publication read almost exclusively by people in the 15-30 age bracket – and when asked about student tuition fees Corbyn is said to have replied: "Yes, there is a block of those that currently have a massive debt, and I'm looking at ways that we could reduce that, ameliorate that, lengthen the period of paying it off, or some other means of reducing that debt burden" (Gray, 2017). Thus, whilst not actually promising to scrap tuition fees, he gave the impression that he would like to do so: he was being 'economical with the truth.' Luckily for Corbyn (and the rest of the UK) he did not win the general election, but his mealy-mouthed manipulation of meaning must surely serve as a warning of what we might expect were he ever to attain power.

The second example is of political promises that were subsequently broken: that of the Liberal Democrats' promise not to increase tuition fees should they be elected to power in the 2010 General Election. In the Party's Election Manifesto of that year, it clearly stated that the Liberal Democrats "...will scrap unfair university tuition fees so everyone has the chance to get a degree, regardless of their parents' income" (Liberal Democrats, 2010:33). Once invited into a coalition government with the Conservatives, this electoral promise was conveniently forgotten, and the Liberals supported an increase in student fees.

It is, therefore, the height of hypocrisy to complain that the British electorate were 'conned' into voting for Brexit as they were unaware of all the facts. As stated at the beginning of this book, nobody (either then or now) can be certain of the politico-economic landscape following the UK's departure from the EU. Those who call for a re-run should be aware that they leave themselves open to charges of being anti-democratic, and of helping Brussels by seeding division in the UK – which for politicians who function in a modern Western democracy, must surely be unacceptable?

Whilst the UK population accepts the verdict to leave, many prominent 'remainers' (possibly those with most to lose financially from 'Brexit') appear incapable of accepting the result of this democratic referendum; are those who call for another referendum, presumably in the hope that this would reverse the outcome. It is somewhat hypocritical as amongst those calling for people to ignore (or even reverse) the outcome of the referendum are politicians – leaders of major political parties – who did not challenge the democratic process when it suited them, and have done so only when they felt that the people 'got it wrong' the last time. In the 2005 UK General Election (the last fought by Tony Blair), Labour won power by 9,567,589 votes to the 8,784,915 votes polled by the Conservatives. This gave Labour a win by 782, 674 votes, on a 61.4% electoral turnout (UK Political Info, 2005). Compare these figures with those for the recent EU referendum, in which the 'leavers' polled 17,410,742 votes, compared with 16,141,241 for 'remain', giving a lead of 1,269,501 votes in favour of leaving

– based on a turnout of 72%. How people such as Tony Blair (who was happy to accept power on the basis of such a small margin in 2005) can suggest that the Brexit process be halted is difficult to understand, other than it shows he believes in democracy as and when it suits him to do so.

This is not the way that democracy works: otherwise after every General Election, those who were unhappy with the result could immediately call for another election, based on the fact that there were many people who did not agree with the outcome. When it suits people such as Blair to talk about democracy they are happy to abide by the decision of the electorate; as soon as the public votes for what he thinks is wrong, he complains vociferously, and attempts to get the electorate to 'rise up' against Brexit (BBC, 2017; Mason, 2017; Swinford and Watson, 2017). Blair claimed that "... the people voted without knowledge of the terms of Brexit. As these terms become clear, it is their right to change their mind" (Swinford, 2017a:4). By this logic, one could equally suggest that had people known Blair was going to involve the country in a war in Iraq if re-elected, would it have been appropriate to have re-run the 2001 general election as Blair made no mention of it in the Labour Manifesto, yet subsequently involved the country in a war in which hundreds of UK service personnel lost their lives? In making remarks such as these, Blair does not see that he is a large part of the problem: he makes the country appear divided, and the current EU negotiators seize on this message to try to make Brexit as prolonged, painful, and costly as possible. The danger is that Blair's comments will become a self-fulfilling prophesy, and that the UK will suffer, but only as a consequence of his betrayal of the referendum.

These comments by Blair are at best ill-judged and irresponsible, at worst tantamount to inciting civil disobedience – something that he would not have tolerated when Prime Minister. In April 2017, during the run-up to the General Election, Blair is reported to have said that people should vote for any MP who opposes Brexit, and that includes possibly voting Conservative not Labour (Wright, 2017:11). Lord Malloch-Brown (Chairman of the anti-Brexit "Best for Britain" group) spent the last months of 2017 in discussions with other like-minded groups – such as "Open Britain" – the group backed by Peter Mandleson, over how to oppose Brexit. With regard to Blair, Malloch-Brown said to *The Sunday Times*: "I respect his message and pretty much fully agree with it, but I think he is the wrong person to deliver it" (Kinchen, 2018:29).

Despite being largely dismissed as 'yesterday's man', Blair continues to seek a role on the world stage, and it would appear that the EU may well be his target of choice, despite the fact that he has come under intense criticism for his apparent dismissal of democracy, even from amongst members of his own political party. Could it be that Blair still has his eye on the Presidency of the EU? If he does, he had better move quickly, or he might find himself President of a shrinking collection of embittered states, the populations of which are increasingly disillusioned with the many corrupt and self-seeking politicians who inhabit the parallel planet that is Brussels. With interventions from people such as Blair and Mandleson, it would appear that there is a rump within the wealthy, liberal/left-wing elites who have still not accepted the fact that the 'Brexit' vote won.

Ill-judged and sometimes simply stupid comments are not the sole preserve of Labour politicians, as evidenced by the post-referendum pronouncements of Philip Hammond, in his role as Chancellor of the Exchequer. In a widely-reported speech, Hammond (who voted 'remain') said that the country faced an economic 'roller-coaster ride', and commented that the public did not "...vote for Brexit to make themselves poorer" (*The Economist*, 2016e: 28; Warner, 2017:2). The new Caretaker leader of the Liberal democrats, Vince Cable, was apparently having secret talks with pro-Remain Tory MPs in June 2017. Many voters are likely to feel a sense of betrayal by the activities of politicians such as Cable, as it is now important that MPs from both sides of the House work together to ensure the best Brexit that can be achieved. It has been suggested that "Voters will not forgive politicians who are indulging in shabby games rather than supporting the Government in delivering on the referendum result" (Hope and Johnson, 2017:9).

In October 2017, the veteran Conservative Europhile Kenneth Clarke waded into the debate. Of all the senior politicians with an opinion on the EU, Clarke has been consistently pro-EU since the UK joined in 1973; whilst it could be argued that he is wrong in his assessment, it could never be argued that he is unprincipled. His intervention was a mixture of resignation and 'last ditch' defiance: he told the *BBC Today*: "It is not the aim of my amendments [to the EU Withdrawal Bill] to reverse leaving..." but as he pointed out, Parliament has the final say in approving legislative bills (Pickard, 2017:3). This Bill was to have been debated in October 2017, but has been withdrawn from Parliamentary business due to the growing opposition, and the subsequent likelihood that the government might not secure its approval (Rayner et.al., 2017:1). The latest example of anti-democratic interference was reported in *The Sunday Telegraph*, which claimed that four out of the ten Commissioners on the UK's electoral Commission had "...made public statements criticising the pro-Brexit campaign or backing calls for the result to be overturned..." As Jacob Rees-Mogg pointed out: "This is very serious as the regulator of elections must be impartial" (Malnick, 2018: 1).

At the same time, the more emotive wings of the 'remain resistance army', led by men such as Blair (and other London-based fellow-travelers) appear to be going out of their way to encourage people to push for a second referendum – possibly to get the 'right' result next time (Mason and Elgot, 2017). Possible attempts to derail Brexit include intelligent economists (Smith, 2017:4), who suggest that the government still has no idea of what it is doing, and that "...we know what the government is against, but not yet what it is for..." This is a fair comment, but one that, nevertheless weakens our negotiating position with the EU – possibly this is of little concern to Smith, as he was an avowed 'remainer' – although it should be of concern to everyone ('remainer' or 'leaver') as the more divided the country appears, the more the EU will try to insist on crippling economic terms on which to begin to negotiate the UK's continuing trade relations.

Various other 'retired' politicians who should know better are also proclaiming publicly the need for a re-think of Brexit. One such intervention was by ex-Prime Minister John Major – the man who signed the *Maastricht Treaty*, which arguably led us to the position we are in today. In his ill-judged intervention in February 2017, Major complained that "... the British people have been led to expect a future outside the EU that seems to be unreal and over-optimistic..." suggesting that: "Obstacles are brushed aside as of no consequence, whilst opportunities are inflated beyond any reasonable expectation of delivery" (Stewart, 2017). Major is one of a number of individuals who seem to have forgotten history and their own involvement in its making. He is quoted as having said (in November 2016) that there was a "...perfectly credible case..." for a "...second referendum..." (Swinford and Hughes, 2016:8), thus undermining the position of the Prime Minister and a number of key Ministers involved in the Brexit discussions. It is interesting to recall that, when in 1993 Major faced continued opposition from a group of his own backbenchers led by Sir William Cash (later to be known as the "Maastricht rebels") over closer EU integration, he famously described them as 'bastards' for opposing him. As he is effectively doing the same now to another Conservative Prime Minister, would he also describe himself as a 'bastard' for his lack of loyalty?

It is interesting to speculate what the attitude of these wreckers would have been had the Brexit vote gone the other way? One suspects that we would have been subject to long lectures on the will of the people being paramount. In many ways the likes of Blair, Major, Hesseltine and Mandelson and the metropolitan elites, are acting as if they were African Dictators, and refusing to accept the results of an election, feeling that they know 'what is best' for the British people. The way to deal those who wish to halt Brexit, and/or call for a second referendum, is to say 'no'. The decision to leave was arrived at by an openly democratic process, and as with every general election that has preceded it (and the 1975 EEC referendum), the decision is final and irrevocable. Consider, for example, a scenario in which the numbers had been reversed... ie. one million-plus vote to remain. Would the winners have then agreed that there should have been another referendum? Democracy hinges on voting, and voting has taken place.

Unfortunately it would appear that such unelected people do have the power to potentially thwart the outcome of a democratic referendum; it was reported in April 2018 that a cross-Party group of MPs, Peers and other 'remainers' were launching a concerted effort (underpinned by a reported £1 million fund) to thwart the will of the people, with the objective of uniting all the remain groups into a cohesive pressure group that advocates giving people the chance to vote on the outcome of negotiations, and to reverse the decision to leave. In an interview with *The Daily Telegraph*: Sir William Cash observed: "They are completely defying the British people who made a decision which was given to them by parliament itself. The latest polling says 65 per cent of the British people do not want a second referendum…" (McCann, 2018:8). In their latest contribution to the nation's future well-being the Lords blocked Theresa May's 'Brexit Bill', on 19th April, 2018, and in so doing, called into question the government's commitment to leave the Customs union.

As Gavin (2018), reported: "…a cross-party alliance of Lords, including Tory rebels, put forward an amendment to the Government's EU Withdrawal Bill and voted by 348 to 225 in favour of changing the landmark legislation. In a major defeat for Mrs May's Government, the amendment…would compel her to at least attempt to negotiate terms for a customs union arrangement, the report back to parliament." The Conservative Peer, Lord Forsyth, commented that the latest sabotage by the Lords was "…an exercise by Remainers in the House who refuse to accept the verdict of the British people…" and he branded it an attempt to create division and confusion in the Commons' (Gavin, 2018). In doing this, the Lords (an unelected, and therefore non-democratic body), are playing with fire, as they appear to have set themselves in direct opposition to the democratic decision of the public to leave. This brings their abolition one step closer.

Brexit: KBO

CHAPTER 6 | THE IMMEDIATE FUTURE

6.1. Introduction

Despite the expressed will of the people, the process of exiting the EU is fraught with difficulties – not least of which is the opposition to a mix of continued access to the Single Market, coupled with restricted movement of people: many EU nations – for whatever reason – are unlikely to make the process easy, and are highly likely to block all efforts to 'square this circle.' As *The Economist* pointed out:

"In the 13 months since the referendum, the awesome complexity of ending a 44-year *political and economic* union [author's italics] has become clear. Britain's position on everything from mackerel stocks to nuclear waste is being worked out by a civil service whose headcount has fallen by nearly a quarter in the past decade and which has not negotiated a trade deal of its own in a generation" (*The Economist*, 2017c: 11).

The Economist has apparently accepted that the EU is both an economic and political union yet the idea of a political union (the "United States of Europe") has never been put formally to the electorate of Member states. Thus, one can only conclude that either the journal does not understand what has been going on for the last 40 years (highly unlikely), or it feels that the opinions of voters are irrelevant as such issues are best settled by national governments without involving their electorate – possibly indicative of an establishment-supporting journal.

The EU negotiators have to be careful, however, as of the two scenarios generally postulated (a 'hard' or 'soft' Brexit), it is argued that the 'hard' alternative would hurt all concerned, although there are those that consider it their best option; Theresa May is often quoted as saying that 'no agreement is better that a bad agreement', and no agreement would lead to a 'hard' Brexit, which would basically mean that negotiations had broken down, and that all future trading relationships between the UK and the EU would be based on WTO tariff terms of trade – a prospect that would be far less attractive to the EU than it would to the UK – for the simple reason that we buy more from the them than they buy from us. This would also mean that the UK could impose entry restrictions to prevent EU citizens coming to live and work in the UK – unless they have previously acquired a job, are sponsored by a UK company, and have been issued with a work visa. At one stroke, we could considerably reduce the number of immigrants into the UK.

Bearing in mind the political realities, 'negotiations' with the UK over Brexit are likely to be protracted, unrealistic, and unworkable, which is only to be expected: the former Greek Finance Minister (Yanis Varoufakis) who had extensive experience of 'negotiating' with the EU, warned that the EU will exploit any 'internal political friction in the UK' and will 'drown negotiations in the minutiae of the so-called divorce' (Editorial, 2017b:19).

The same editorial piece noted that the price of the 'divorce' keeps going up: "The EU is now expanding its financial settlement to include "political" commitments, such as assistance to refugees. The goal is to waste Britain's energy fighting one battle in the hope that it will surrender the wider war." After all, as pointed out earlier, the EU has no motivation to make any concessions to the UK – quite the opposite, as any concessions would merely encourage anti-EU parties in other member states.

Those who criticise the government for not making clear the precise terms agreed thus far over Brexit negotiations should perhaps bear in mind that we were in a similar situation in the course of our initial negotiations over membership. When the Government White Paper on UK accession to the EEC was first debated (February 1970), there was equal uncertainty. On 24th February 1970, the following exchange took place between Mr John Mendelson MP, and Mr Michael Stewart MP, Secretary of State for Foreign and Commonwealth Affairs; Mr. John Mendelson asked: "If my right hon. Friend is so anxious to impress upon the House the large area of uncertainty about any assumptions, how, during the negotiations, will he insist on minimum conditions to safeguard the interests of the people of this country?" The reply from Mr. Stewart was: ".... When we come to negotiations, it is equally true that nobody could nail down to the last degree what exactly the results would be. In the event, and I think that everybody who has studied this matter knows it, this must be a qualitative judgment." (*Hansard*, 1970a: 1000). And this was against a backdrop of negotiations undertaken by previous countries when they became members, and when there was goodwill and encouragement on behalf of those existing members. How much more difficult and uncertain, therefore, to negotiate withdrawal (a process that has never been previously undertaken), and when then other members of the club are unwilling to come to an accommodation, as they do not wish us to leave.

6.2. The 'Divorce Bill'

The so-called 'Divorce Bill' is basically EU-inspired blackmail, as it was made clear to the UK negotiating team that until the UK agrees to a 'leaving' payment, there is no possibility of discussing the basis of future trading relations (Foster, 2017:9). In September 2017, Michel Barnier (the European Commission's Chief Negotiator) made a speech in which he said that the UK must "... settle its accounts..." (Crisp and Maidment, 2017:6) before a free trade deal was even discussed, let alone agreed. Whilst the UK wished talks about the process of exiting the EU and the new EU-UK relationship to be discussed in tandem, the EU rejected this (Foster, 2017:9). It is richly ironic that on the one hand the EU negotiators and Heads of State have threatened that unless the UK agrees over 'reparations' and the future rights of EU citizens, they will not begin to talk about trade; at the same time, a Dutch politician, Guy Verhofstadt, the Chief negotiator at the European Parliament, accused the UK of 'blackmail' over a supposed threat to withdraw co-operation over security (Foster, 2017:9).

Barnier was reported as insisting that the UK continues paying into EU funds for up to four years after it has left, based on an estimated "Brexit Bill" of €60-billion. As Foster (2017:9), writing in *The Telegraph* noted: "The aim of the payments would be to help smooth over the €10bn-a-year black hole left in the EU budgets by Britain's departure from the EU, which could see richer countries like Germany and France paying more, or poorer countries, like Poland and Hungary receiving less." In return, the EU would promise a deal that would "... govern future trade relations..." between the UK and the EU. The EU Commission appears to have learnt nothing over the last year or so: a major reason why people voted 'leave' was that they no longer trusted the bureaucrats who ran the EU – yet these same bureaucrats are asking for €60-billion in return for vague promises relating to unspecified trade deals in the future! The chief cheerleader in the anti-UK camp, Juncker, could not help but inject his spiteful contribution into the debate, saying that the EU must be "...intransigent ..." in denying UK firms access to the SEM if there is no agreement over the free movement of people (Foster and Day, 2016:18) – the reasons for the EU's insistence on this have already been made clear in Chapter 3.4 "The Free Movement of People."

The first inklings of the insistence of the EU over an early 'exit' payment by the UK had emerged in early 2017, when Britain set the date for triggering Article 50; as far as can be ascertained, an 'exit' payment is not mentioned in the EU treaty or *Article 50*. Despite Juncker's comments to the contrary, there is no reason why membership of the EU cannot be likened to membership of a golf club – having given notice, and paid ones' dues up to the end of the month, one then leaves, and has no further financial obligations. However, the EU does not view membership in the same way, and despite there being no evidence on which to base their position, they insist that that one cannot simply leave the EU as if it were a club. They are wrong. There is nothing in the EU treaty to this effect: other than insisting on a two-year 'negotiation period', the *Treaty* does not go into detail – presumably because when it was written it was assumed that no country would ever wish to leave. In an insightful Working Paper published by the Brussels-based economic think-tank 'Bruegel', Darvas et. al. (2017:1) suggest that the 'golf club' versus 'divorce' viewpoint is basically what divides opinion on the monies owed by the UK on leaving. They point out that:

"The size of the Brexit bill will depend on fundamental political compromises and choices. The key question is whether one considers Brexit to be a cancellation of a club membership or a divorce. In the former case, the UK would have no claims on any EU asserts but would still need to pay its outstanding membership fees. In the latter case, both assets and liabilities would have to be split."

This is the key issue, around which most of the arguments appear to have focused thus far. The message coming from Brussels appears to be in terms of immediate payment of outstanding fees, it is apparently regarded as a club by the EU negotiators who insisted that the UK pays what it owes before moving talks on to future issues – Barnier's demand that the UK "... settle its accounts..." Based on this understanding, it is likely that the matter could be settled relatively painlessly. However, whilst insisting that the UK pays its outstanding 'club' fees (a rather over-inflated bill), the EU appears to be also regarding the process as a divorce by insisting that the UK makes additional contributions to areas from which it will not benefit in the future – a division of liabilities, but without a simultaneous division of assets. By any divorce terms, this is unacceptable, and it is this 'have your cake and eat it' mentality that is increasingly annoying many UK citizens, whom, with a British sense of 'fair play' see it as totally unjustified.

As a member of an organisation that has financial commitments many years into the future, it is perhaps only fair that the UK contributes to those areas for which it has already promised (but not yet made) a contribution. By the same token, the EU should seek to refund the UK funds that have been paid towards a common cause, but which have not yet been used: such as the thousands of bottles of wine stored by the EU (estimated at some 42,000 bottles), for which the UK has contributed funds, but will be unable to enjoy the wine after we leave. Reports suggest that the UK is insisting (not unreasonably), that a percentage of these bottles should be returned (Mercer, 2016) – probably to the UK Parliament for entertainment purposes.

There is also the question of the collection of artwork, purchased at great expense, which currently adorns the walls of many official buildings, not to mention the jointly-purchased office furniture and equipment such as computers, televisions, printers, in addition to joint purchases for the purpose of entertaining foreign dignitaries such as dining furniture, crockery and glassware. The list of such assets is almost endless, and if the EU really does insist on a 'divorce' then these assets should be divided up, rather than the UK being given the liabilities (the Brexit bill) and the EU retaining all the assets. It is to be hoped that the cost of such assets will be at least deducted from the final 'divorce bill', although in view of the way the negotiations are being conducted, it is more likely that they will want everything in order to weaken us, and so doing provide a lesson for any other country that might wish to leave. In the final consideration, is it a question of cancelling our membership of the club, or of a divorce? The EU cannot have it both ways, despite their desire to do so. The EU negotiators are so stupid that they have not apparently realised that taking such an uncompromising hard line with the UK is likely to send exactly the wrong message to current EU members with significant 'leave' voters, and to those countries that are contemplating joining.

There is no reason why we should continue to contribute to the EU budget, over and above honouring our existing commitments. We will no longer be a member of the club, so why should we continue to pay membership fees? In effect, the so-called 'divorce settlement' is more akin to the reparations payments imposed by the French on Germany through the *Treaty of Versailles* at the end of WWI – and there is much evidence to show how this ultimately led to the rise of extremist parties such as the NSDAP (Nazi) Party. Without wishing to push the simile too far, it is interesting to note that over the last two decades there has been a noticeable growth in 'populist' (nationalist) parties throughout Europe, most (if not all) of which are predominately anti-EU (refer back to Chapter 5.2 "European Opposition to the EU"). As Allister Heath recently noted in his column in *The Daily Telegraph*, the unreasonable demands are causing more friction within the UK:

"Forget Leavers or Remainers: the real, unbridgeable split is now between those who are outraged by the Eurocrat's preposterous demands and those who shamefully, have decided to take the EU's side….Its latest preposterous demands – that we should hand over €100-billion for the privilege of regaining our self-government and that we can, in effect, never really leave – are so belligerent, so absurdly punitive that they will be remembered as a seminal moment in the hardening of British opinion" (Heath, 2017:18).

In the final analysis, the size of the payment is still unclear for a number of reasons: including the exchange rate (Euros to pounds sterling), the length of time over which payments should be made, and the specific liabilities for which the UK has accepted responsibility. According to The Institute for Government (IfG), the deal agreed in December 2017 "…did not contain an exact figure, though at the time, UK officials estimated a potential bill of £35-39-billion…." The Institute also noted that:

"The UK's Office for Budget Responsibility (OBR) set out detailed estimates of what the UK would pay in its Economic and Fiscal Outlook report, published alongside the Chancellor's Spring Statement. That set out a total bill of €41.4bn

(£37.1bn), extending out to 2064 as pension liabilities fall due. But it also makes clear that around half consist of payments the UK will make during the transition phase. The OBR estimates net payments under the financial settlement of €18.5bn (£16.4bn) in 2019 and 2020, during the transition, followed by net payments of €7.6bn in 2021, €5.8bn (2022) €3.1bn (2023) and €1.7bn (2024) before falling away to €0.2bn in 2028. The liabilities, net of assets, that then remain to be paid amount to a total of €2.7bn over the period 2021–45" (IfG, 2018).

6.3. The Transition Period

The latest to be apparently agreed is that the UK will come out of the EU gradually – a so-called 'transition period'; this is designed to allow businesses to adjust to the new working arrangements with the EU. The fact that the EU negotiators wanted such an arrangement suggests that they have no intention of giving the UK 'Free Trade' status following Brexit; thus, the position has been decided even before so-called negotiations are concluded. It should be obvious to all concerned that the real reason the EU wants a 'transition period' is that as they are preparing for a UK exit without a trade agreement, their exporters to the UK will have to re-adjust their trading focus: the 21 month 'transition period' demanded by Barnier will be necessary to ensure that EU exporters do not suffer unduly. As noted by Boffey and Stewart (2018):

"During that period the UK will effectively remain a member of the single market and the customs union under the jurisdiction of the European court of justice, but without any say in the EU's rules. The EU's chief negotiator, Michel Barnier, has claimed that 31 December 2020 is the most practical end date for the transition as it would dovetail with the end of the bloc's seven-year budget and avoid the opening up of discussions on payments in addition to the UK's £35-£39bn divorce settlement."

This would put the UK at a considerable disadvantage, as effectively, we would be forced to remain EU members for another two years – considerably increasing the danger of a 'coup' by the 'remainers' as detailed earlier. Furthermore, if we were subject to EU law during the transition period, then we could not begin trading new non-EU markets, as the current legislation prevents this. Once again, the EU is employing every trick in the book to make life difficult for us, to ensure the maximum financial payment is extracted, and that our international trade suffers. It is to be hoped that other countries are observing the true face of the EU, and any that have desires to join, should consider their position carefully before putting pen to paper.

Following the agreement over the 'transition period', Barnier appeared to take great delight in announcing that "British citizens and European citizens of the 27 who arrive during the transition period will receive the same rights and guarantees as those who arrived before the day of Brexit" (Boffey, *et. al.*, 2018). This is understood to mean that freedom of movement will continue for another two years: a key EU requirement, as detailed in chapter 3.4 ("The Free Movement of People).

The deal also meant that whilst the UK remained in the CU for another two years, we would have no involvement in any decision-making. Whilst this might be portrayed as a negative consequence, it will make little or no difference in the long run, as such decisions are either made behind closed doors (The EU Commission), or as a consequence of majority voting. Either way, even when a full member, the UK has had very little opportunity to influence EU policy – so there will be little noticeable change during the transition period. Jacob Rees-Mogg MP, called the transition agreement unsatisfactory and said it was "…hard to see what points the government has won." His colleague, Ian Duncan-Smith MP told the BBC: "There does seem to be a real concern … It appears that at least through the implementation period nothing will change and I think that will be a concern and the government clearly has to deal with that because a lot of MPs are very uneasy about that right now."

6.4. Free Trade or Tariffs?

Being tied into deals brokered on our behalf by Brussels is to our considerable disadvantage, as the inefficiency and corruption of the Brussels machinery (Harris, 2017) tends to mitigate against competitive outcomes of trade negotiations and inter-market efficiencies. As with most things over which the EU has control, decisions are ultimately subject to political (rather than economic or logical) considerations. Rather than any trading agreement being a consequence of the petitions of EU- and/or UK-based businesses, the decision will most likely be made by the EU Commission, which seeks to use trading relations as a means of punishing the UK for having the temerity to leave the club (Lilico, 2014). This is the key issue, around which most of the arguments appear to have focused thus far.

Based on the attitudes, animosity and unwillingness on the part of the EU negotiators to compromise that have characterised negotiations thus far, we have to assume that by 29th March 2019, the UK will be forced to walk away from further 'negotiations.' If we were to leave the EU without having come to any agreement over trade, we would lose its access to the SEM and CU, and commercial relationships between the EU and the UK would, for the foreseeable future, be based on WTO guidelines. However, such a scenario would also mean that the UK would also be free to make its own bilateral trade deals. Thus, in the short-medium term at least, if both the EU and the UK were to trade on WTO terms (a 'hard' Brexit), the UK would be free to explore (and implement) bilateral trade deals with non-EU countries.

The UK currently trades with many countries and regions that are not members of the EU – India, China, Africa, and Latin America – growing regions of the world, with large populations, and in which there are considerable opportunities for British goods. We must increase our trade with these regions, and where possible negotiate bilateral trading agreements; indeed, since the election of Donald Trump as President of the USA, the process has already begun with the visit of the UK Prime Minister to Washington to discuss trade deals. What is to stop us from increasing our trade with these regions, and where possible negotiating bilateral trading agreements? Hard on the heels of talks with the Americans, Theresa May concluded a visit to Turkey, during which agreements were made for UK defence sales to that country, and medium-term post-Brexit bilateral trading relations were discussed.

There are many permutations of the ways in which future UK trading relations might be developed, but as a starting point all hinge on the extent to which the UK can maintain continued access to the Single European Market and Customs Union, whilst securing independence of action to negotiate bi-lateral trade deals with countries outside the EU. There are two possible extreme outcomes for future trading with the EU:

Outcome 1: "Continued Free SEM/CU Access"

The UK leaves the EU, but retains current access to the SEM and CU (with EU exporters having similar access to UK markets). The majority of UK businesses want this outcome; for example in a survey of 'What UK business wants from Brexit', the *Financial Times* found a large majority in favour of maintenance of the current trading arrangements. Typical comments were that made by the organisation Enterprise Nation, which represents around 71,000 small businesses:

"Small firms don't want borders and time-consuming border checks. Hold-ups at borders could be disastrous for British food producers, for example, with products with a short shelf-life. For those operating in a world where we expect orders to be fulfilled very quickly, border checks would put them at a big disadvantage. Staying in the single market, would mean less bureaucracy to worry about — like different VAT regimes or import duties" (Wasik and Gordon, 2017).

However, the Federation of Small Businesses was more sanguine in their assessment, balancing the problems of leaving the CU with the opportunities that real Free Trade represents:

"We would be deeply concerned about the impact on small businesses of leaving the customs union. Having said that, we recognise there are potential longer-term opportunities that leaving it could bring in terms of making trade deals with countries outside the EU. There has been talk of an associate membership of the EU customs union. We urgently need to understand what models are being considered so we can engage with members and provide real frontline insight on how to minimise the burdens and costs of any additional customs checks, or the potential application of rules of origin, on small businesses" (Wasik and Gordon, 2017).

The majority of EU businesses that deal with the UK want to maintain free trade: typical is the boss of BMW, who was quoted as saying that a free trade deal is essential for the well-being of the car industry in both the UK and Germany. He wishes to produce BMW-owned cars (which include the "Mini" and "Rolls-Royce") in electric versions (which BMW regards as the future of automobiles) in the UK, but the lack of a free trade deal might make that difficult. BMW relies on the UK as a major market, and as he explains: "What is clear is we need free trade. We can't invest into the future if you don't have any free trade agreements. If everyone plays hard it will be difficult; if there is nothing, then probably both sides would lose" (Collingridge, 2017).

Outcome 2: "No deal" – Trade by Tariff

Despite what is said by EU politicians about denying the UK access to the SEM and CU, EU businesses involved in international trading are overwhelmingly opposed to trading on WTO terms, as this would be to their disadvantage more than to the UK. As shown in Table 4. there is a healthy level of trade between the UK and various member countries of the EU, but it also shows that with the exception of Italy we import more from the EU that we export to them. There is an overall trade imbalance, with EU countries exporting to us more than we do to them. Sir James Dyson, a passionate 'leaver', pointed out that the EU "...is small and the real growing and exciting markets are outside Europe" (Pearson, 2016c:13). The fact that the UK has the ability, knowledge, Commonwealth network, and experience of trading outside the EU must surely act as some form of incentive to Brussels to support a free trade arrangement? If not, there exists a real danger that the UK will drastically reduce its trade with the EU, and switch its export (and import) focus elsewhere.

The 'no deal' scenario would mean that the UK could enter into a variety of trade deals with countries outside the EU – something that is currently prohibited by Brussels. Contrary to popular opinion, the EU is not our number one trading partner – that is the USA: in 2015, the UK's trade with the USA gave us a huge trading surplus of some £40-billion (Burton and Salmon, 2017). By the following year, UK exports to the USA had grown further, and were now valued at US\$60.4- billion – representing 14.8% of total UK exports (Workman, 2018). See table 5 below:

Table 5: Top 15 UK Export Markets (2016)		
Export Destination	Value of total UK Exports (US $ billion)	Percentage of total UK Exports (by value)
USA	60.4	14.8
Germany	43.6	10.7
France	25.9	6.3
Netherlands	25.6	6.3
Ireland	22.9	5.6
Switzerland	18.9	4.6
China	18.0	4.4
Belgium	15.8	3.9
Italy	13.1	3.2
Spain	12.7	3.1
United Arab Emirates	9.0	2.2
Hong Kong	8.8	2.2
Japan	6.4	1.6
Canada	6.2	1.5
Sweden	6.1	1.5
Totals	US $ 293.4 billion	71.9 %

Source: based on Workman (2018)

Assuming that at best, trading with the EU will be difficult over the next 5-10 years, we should begin now to look for non-EU trading partners to replace any shortfall – something that The Department for Exiting the European Union, The Department for International Trade and The Department of Trade & Industry should address as a priority issue. Within the short/medium term, there has to be a concerted effort by the Government Ministries mentioned to ensure that they acquire the knowledge that will be needed in the future to negotiate independently on the international stage.

By all accounts, these departments are currently devising a strategy as part of the negotiations that have been taking place since the triggering of article 50 in March 2017, and are working towards maintaining the best possible future trading relations with EU member states. What is less likely, however, is the extent to which they are focused on the development of such links outside the

EU area; it is unclear whether they have yet developed a strategic focus, and have been able to examine potential markets in sufficient depth to be of use to prospective exporters and companies seeking business partners.

Thus, control over foreign economic and trading relations is a key element of the UK's future on the international stage: and under current EU legislation, this can only be achieved through leaving the EU. Once this has happened, we shall be free to make trade deals of our own choosing, without the dead hand of Brussels bureaucracy and the agreement of twenty-seven other states. Commentators such as Erixon (2017) conclude that "A free-trade deal between the UK and the EU can be expected for a simple reason: neither side can afford to throw away huge volumes of trade." As he explains, a free-trade deal with Britain "...is certainly in the interests of Spain and Italy, who run a trade surplus with Britain. For Germany, which exports €50-billion more to the UK than Brits buy from Germans, it's a no-brainer. Cars, chemicals and machinery – these strong export sectors for Germany are all at risk if Britain copies EU tariffs on cars and imposes its own regulation on hazardous chemicals. And French farmers and winemakers will lobby just as hard: they don't want to see British duties on Beaujolais and Camembert." Interestingly, there are some UK manufacturers that are less enamoured with EU free trade advantages, as they feel that the benefits of the single market are far outweighed by the increased bureaucracy emanating from Brussels. Lord Bamford (Chairman of JCB) was recently quoted as having said that "...the cost of European regulations to business is so burdensome that even leaving the single market would be a 'price worth paying' to escape the EU diktat" (Editorial, 2016f: 25).

It is unrealistic for the UK to attempt to 'negotiate' trade agreements for the post-Brexit period; from the point of view of many EU politicians (and many UK citizens), the UK should now leave at the earliest opportunity. Indeed, many in both the UK and the EU wonder why article 50 was not triggered the day after Theresa May's accession to the office of Prime Minister. Once we leave, the UK will be free to make trade deals of its own choosing, without having to seek the agreement of twenty-seven other states (Garcia-Herrero and Xu, 2016). Interestingly, the process has already begun: in October 2016, an Australian Trade delegation arrived in the UK to begin post-Brexit trade bilateral trade talks (Wallace, 2016c). Following his election to Presidency of the USA, Donald Trump indicated that he would look favourably on making a Free Trade deal with the UK, and possibly scrapping plans for a free trade deal with the European Union. This has reportedly sent EU leaders into a panic (Davies, 2016), especially as President Trump is also reported as having said that: "No longer will we enter into these massive transactions with many countries that are thousands of pages long and which no one from our country even reads or understands" (Swinford, 2016g). According to the UK Foreign

Office, as a consequence of the visit to the USA by Foreign Secretary Boris Johnston, the UK is likely to be 'first in line' for negotiating bilateral trade deals with the new Trump administration.

As Ward noted in his briefing paper to the House of Commons, there is a wide range of tariff payments for goods imported into the EU from non-EU countries, which are required to "... pay the EU's common external tariff, unless there is a free trade agreement or preferential trade agreement. The tariff rate differs between goods. While on average EU tariffs are low, they are high for some products, especially agricultural products. The trade-weighted average EU tariff for non-agricultural products was 2.3 % in 2014 and 8.5% for agricultural products." (Ward, 2017: 8)

Table: 6: Average EU Import Tariff, by Product Type (as a % of Value)	
Product Type	**Average % Tariff**
Dairy products	35.5
Sugars and confectionery	23.6
Beverages and tobacco	19.6
Animal products	15.7
Cereals and preparations	12.8
Fish and fish products	12.0
Clothing	11.5
Fruit, vegetables and plants	10.5
Textiles	6.5
Coffee, tea	6.1
Oilseed, fats and oils	5.6
Chemicals	4.5
Transport equipment	4.3
Leather, footwear etc	4.1
Other agricultural products	3.6
Electrical machinery	2.8
Other manufactures	2.6
Petroleum	2.5
Minerals and metals	2.0
Non-electrical machinery	2.0
Wood, paper etc	1.9
Cotton	0.0

Source: adapted from Ward (2017) "Statistics on UK-EU Trade" Briefing Paper Number 7851 (19th December). House of Commons Library, p.8

Thus, in the event of no trade deal being reached, and both the EU and UK living with a 'hard' Brexit in the short-medium term at least, the most likely scenario would be that of mutual reciprocity. As discussed earlier, if the EU were to place tariffs on UK imports, then the UK would have the right to place equal tariff levels on EU imports into the UK. As we import far more (in terms of both volume and value) from the EU that we export (refer back to table 2.1.), any 'tit-for-tat' tariff war would ultimately harm the EU more than the UK. German car manufacturers would undoubtedly lobby the German government, as would German manufacturers of machinery, pharmaceuticals, and electronic equipment.

As the Office for National Statistics (ONS, 2018) noted: "Motor vehicles and parts is the largest product group by value of exports: the UK exported £18-billion of motor vehicles (and trailers) to the EU in 2016. The next largest product group exported to the EU is chemicals and chemical products, £15-billion in 2016." Assuming that import tariffs will operate in the future, this would mean that in terms of our largest export category to the EU, UK exporters would be required to pay around 4.3% (by value), and would not be subject to the highest level of tariffs – which are reserved for agricultural and food-related products, and which range from dairy products (including cheese) at 35.5%, to 'beverages and tobacco' (which presumable includes wine) at 19.6%. French exporters of wine, cheese and fruit – respectively 19.6%, 35.5% and 10.5% tariff levies – would suffer, as would those EU exporters who supply the UK with a myriad of food, food-related, beverages, and clothing products, which would be subject to the top tariff rates.

6.5. Northern Ireland

In yet another attempt to 'muddy the waters', and draw the fractious and protracted negotiations out still further, the EU let it be known that a major sticking point with regard to future relations would be the status of Northern Ireland. One argument is that this forms a special case, as it is the only part of the UK that shares a land border with an EU country – in this case the Republic of Ireland (Eire) – and should, therefore, be the subject of slightly different terms of reference to the remainder of the UK. The counter argument is that Northern Ireland is an integral part of the UK, and that should be regarded as such in any Brexit agreement – specifically with regard to trade. As an editorial in *The Daily Telegraph* put it bluntly:

"It must have escaped the notice of the EU's negotiators, but Northern Ireland is part of the United Kingdom. Michel Barnier and his Brussels cohorts have no business dictating to this country how to preserve its territorial integrity" (Editorial, 2018b:17)

Once again Tony Blair has seen fit to intervene in areas where his contribution (such as it is) is most definitely neither required nor productive. In yet another emotive appear based on his version of the facts, in an interview on Radio Four's *'Today'* programme, he said that it was: "…sickening…" that people were prepared "…to sacrifice peace in Northern Ireland on the altar of Brexit" (Radio Four, 2018). Once again Blair was intervening in a manner designed to aid the 'remainers', except this time he was stirring up dangerous Sectarian divisions in his attempt to find favour with Brussels. The *Good Friday Agreement* was between the Irish and British governments, and was nothing to do with the EU; as Charles Moore commented: "Only Blair is capable of such 'magical thinking' that he can turn the largest vote for anything in British history into a threat to democracy" (Moore, 2018: 16).

The issue is basically very simple: both the UK and Irish governments do not want a 'hard' border (ie. border controls) between the two countries: principally because the high volume of trade that crosses both ways on a daily basis. Not only does Eire rely on Northern Ireland as a major destination market for its exports, but in addition it uses ports such as Belfast as routes through which to ship goods to the remainder of the UK, and in many cases, on to the Continent or further afield. Similarly, the UK (and especially Northern Ireland) sells considerable quantities of goods and services to Ireland, customs checks would be highly counter-productive. Regardless of the outcome of London-Brussels negotiations, as Dublin and London both want a 'virtual' trade border, it would be a relatively simple matter to install such checks that were felt necessary ensure the current level of cross-border traffic is not interrupted. In a perceptive article on the Northern Ireland issue, Lawson (2018:20), suggested that the way forward was simple: we adopt border controls such as exist between the EU and Switzerland – what he referred to as a 'frictionless' border. During the course of an address he gave to the Policy Exchange think tank, the Swiss Chief Negotiator – one Michael Ambühl – mentioned the issue of border controls. According to Lawson, in a private conversation he had with Ambühl after the meeting had finished, the Swiss said:

"We never in Switzerland discussed being in a customs union with the EU. You would find it hard to find any Swiss citizen who thought we should do that. If you are outside the EU, you should take advantage of the greater freedom it brings, especially the freedom to make your own trade treaties. We made a trade deal with China, and the average tariffs between China and Switzerland are now lower than those between China and the EU. If you believe in free trade, that is a good thing."

However, the problem is that Dublin, by dint of its membership of the EU, has to abide by majority decisions made in Brussels. As has been stated earlier in this book, the EU bureaucrats that run Brussels are desperate to punish the UK for wanting to leave, and they (erroneously) see a 'hard' Brexit (with attendant tariffs and border controls), as the best way of achieving their punitive strike. Brussels has indicated, in a move designed to cause maximum trouble, that it could not agree to the UK and Ireland devising some form of border control on a bi-lateral basis. Whilst the UK and Irish governments have had a special relationship ever since the formation of Eire in the 1920s, it would appear that Brussels is out to wreck this. As Moore pointed out, the "…only body trying to harden that border [Eire-UK], obsessed by the dogmatic uniformity of its trade rules, is the EU" (Moore, 2018: 16).

Another tactic is to hint that any return to border controls would also bring back terrorism. Beesley (2018:9), writing in the *Financial Times* suggested that "… fears abound that the UK's departure from the EU will lead to the reinstatement of security posts that were taken down after the Good Friday deal [1998], which would not only disrupt free movement over the 500km frontier that is invisible to the eye, but could also become a target for dissident republican paramilitaries bent on a return to violence." It is hard to see why this should happen, unless the 'paramilitaries' to whom he refers have never really given up violence, and are simply seeking an excuse to return to murder and extortion? Such so-called fears are unjustified, but are surely music to the ears of Brussels as its seeks any way it can to dissuade the UK from leaving the Customs Union.

6.6. Gibraltar

Finally, we come to what is currently regarded as a minor problem, but yet which may turn out to be a major one: the issue of Gibraltar. The 'mischief makers' in Brussels encouraged the government in Madrid to veto UK Brexit proposals, unless they include an undertaking that following the UK's departure, Madrid will have joint control over Gibraltar's airport, in addition to " …greater co-operation on tax fraud and tobacco smuggling" (Stothard, 2018). This is an impossible request to conceed to, and both Madrid and Brussels know it; once again, as with Eire, it is an example of Brussels deliberately placing yet more obstacles in the way of negotiations. If the EU were so concerned about joint sovereignty of the airport, why had they it not raised the issue years ago? Whilst both the UK and Spain were members of the EU (Spain joined in 1986), the issue would have been easier to resolve.

However, if Spain, prodded from behind by Brussels, were to use Gibraltar as a means of vetoing any Brexit agreement for whatever reason, then as Gibraltar remains under UK jurisdiction, there would be an impasse. Would this be so bad for trade and the movement of individuals? Probably not, considering the numerous times that the Spanish authorities have closed the land border with

Gibraltar at La Linea, and/or implemented unnecessary border control checks –both pre- and post-Spanish accession. On a pragmatic level, the government in Madrid is not likely to want to make life difficult for the millions of British tourists that visit Spain each year, nor is it likely to want to draw international attention to the status of Gibraltar, as to do so would invite invidious comparisons with the Spanish-owned enclaves of Ceuta and Melilla in North Africa – both of which are sources of illegal immigration into the EU. Furthermore, Madrid is currently more pre-occupied with its own internal problems, relating to the attempts at independence in Catalunya.

6.7. Conclusions

It is the arrogance, intransigence and corruption of what the former Greek Finance Minister referred to as the 'bullying EU' (Editorial, 2017b:19) that caused many people (the current author included) to vote to leave the EU. The likes of Jean-Claude Juncker should think very carefully about this over the coming months; the British generally do not like complaining or making a fuss in public, however, once pushed too far they become a formidable foe, especially if they consider there is a lack of 'fairness.'

If they begin to see the EU demands as 'unreasonable', they are likely to close ranks against foreign intransigence, and show the meaning of the word 'stubborn'. As Bennett (2017:4), writing in *The Daily Telegraph* observed: "The EU wants Britain to cough up a "single financial settlement", but what would it go towards? The bloc is set to spend around £142-billion this year, so a bumper British bonus would save it from having to worry about how much money it wastes." Set against the phenomenally-expensive cost of maintaining the Brussels workforce, buildings, and the unnecessary activities and commitments that the EU has deemed necessary to justify its existence – not to mention the scandalous expenses claimed by people such as Juncker – it is obvious why the EU needs the British payment to be as large as possible.

As the Conservative UK MEP David Campbell-Bannerman observed in an interview with *The Daily Telegraph*: "If we were too generous with this Brexit bill, what reason would commissioners have to rein in their wasteful, arrogant and out of touch lifestyle? There are no grounds to pay the EU simply to carry on with business as usual" (Crisp, 2017:8). It has obviously never occurred to the Commission that rather than trying to bully the UK into paying for its freedom, it should make significant cuts in its expenditure. In effect, were the EU to withdraw from many of its unnecessary (and highly-expensive) activities – such as its diplomatic representatives – and instead focus its activities on international trade and competition, it could massively reduce its costs, and ask for much less in terms of contributions from member states. Were it to adopt such a strategy, everyone would benefit. Everyone, that is, apart from EU functionaries who might have to adopt a lifestyle more akin to that of the people on whose behalf they purport to work, and that is why it will never happen. In effect, the opposite is more likely, as suggested at the start of this book: the EU is on course for expansion and dominance of Europe – the European 'Superstate', all of which requires money.

It is increasingly obvious that EU politicians such as Juncker want to punish the UK pour encourager les autres – what they are forgetting is that the UK is not beholden to them financially (as are Greece and most of Eastern Europe), has world-wide trading links, and above all, a well-developed sense of democracy and finds the injustices associated with corruption and the abuse of power abhorrent. The UK government appears to be fixated with the objective of securing a post-Brexit free trade deal with the EU; in effect, whilst a free trade deal would be beneficial, it is not worthwhile sacrificing our future for, as there is a big world out there, much of which would be only too happy to come to bilateral trading arrangements with the UK.

In the final analysis, the EU will play the UK for as long as they can, in the hope of extracting as much money from us as they can, based on spurious calculations of outstanding revenue promised in the future, and against which the EU has supposedly allocated expenditure – including the UK's contribution. All this is, of course, nonsense, and is designed to frighten the UK public, and the increasingly-weak UK government into reconsidering their position with regard to Brexit. Even were we to agree to the outrageous 'divorce' terms, this would not guarantee free trade; furthermore as discussed earlier, free trade is something that is possibly of greater benefit to the EU than it is to us. So, in effect, the EU wishes to cripple the UK financially as a punishment for 'leaving', and as a means of discouraging other countries (such as Greece and France) that might be harbouring similar thoughts, after which it might be persuaded to continue trading on terms that broadly favour the EU more than us.

From its attitude during the first year of the two-year notice period, the EU has demonstrated a level of spite and vindictiveness that serves only to reinforce the reasons why the majority voted to leave. We will never come to an amicable agreement over mutually-beneficial terms on which to leave the EU, as the bureaucrats who control the EU will make reaching an agreement as difficult as possible. As previously noted, the problem is not with EU businesses – who by and large want the same as UK businesses – but with the Eurocrats, above all the EU's Chief Negotiator Michel Barnier, who is in danger of becoming a figure of revulsion and derision in the UK and possibly further afield. As *The Spectator* commented recently: "… his constant stonewalling of suggestions put forward by Britain shows the EU in bad light and is a reminder of the freedoms we might enjoy outside the bloc. His tone has been needlessly caustic, and he has seemed to take the Brexit talks as an audition for succeeding Jean-Claude Juncker as president of the European Commission" (Leading Article, 2018).

Whilst Theresa May has suggested that "all sides must be prepared to compromise" (Rayner, 2018:1), the same cannot be said about the deliberately provocative Barnier. Whether his arrogance, rudeness, and duplicity are part of negotiating tactics, or are the mark of the real man inside the urbane outward appearance, is difficult to judge. What is clear, however, is that by proceeding in his current manner he is alienating the British team, and large parts of the UK media and population. What the effect on third party countries will be is even more difficult to calculate, but it cannot have escaped their notice that, like some mafia enforcer, Barnier has decided to be as hostile as he can when dealing with the UK. *The Daily Telegraph* editorial of February 2018 pointed out: "The EU' chief negotiator is clearly out of control and needs to be reined in by those for whom he claims to speak…he insulted the UK at his most recent press conference – patronising us and effectively accusing us of lying – as he defended a ridiculous punishment clause that threatens Britain with grounded flights and blocked trade if we break with EU law during the transition. The transition itself, said Mr Barnier '…is not a given'. In which case, neither is the £39-billion we have generously offered as a divorce settlement" (Editorial, 2018b: 21).

What he is trying to do is bully the UK into accepting a deal that includes continued adherence to the SEM and CU – for, as explained previously, this is the solution that best suits Brussels, although they will never admit such. To this end, rather than adopt a true 'negotiation' approach, based on each side willing to concede certain points until compromise is agreed, Barnier (either of his own volition, or more likely under instructions from Juncker) has decided to pressurise the UK into agreeing to remain in the SEM and CU. In February 2018 he was reported as having said that unless a deal is agreed, the UK will face "…unavoidable barriers to trade…", and in a news conference he attempted to put more pressure on the UK to agree to a SEM/CU deal by saying: "Without the customs union, outside the single market, barriers to trade and goods and services are unavoidable. The time has come to make a choice" (Yorke, 2018:4).

In his desire to make us bend to his objectives as quickly as possible, he has obviously forgotten something that was referred to earlier (Chapter 3.6: "Foreign Trade") – that the 'unavoidable barriers to trade' would apply equally to EU and UK exporters. Rather than accepting such offensive nonsense on face value, the UK team should commission an independent survey that examines the attitude of EU exporters if they were to be faced with the imposition of tariff charges when exporting to the UK. This is the corollary of what Barnier is threatening, and based on previous comments, it is not what EU businesses want, any more than do UK businesses. Thus Barnier, as with other EU officials, is not considering the implications of his threats, as, in the final analysis, were we to leave without some form of Free Trade agreement, EU exporters and not the highly-paid official such as himself would suffer as a consequence of his threat to deny a SEM and CU between the UK and the EU. EU exporters would be likely to focus their wrath on Barnier – after all, he has responsibility for negotiating the most momentous change in the EU since its inception, yet has chosen to squander the opportunities presented through a mixture of arrogance, intimidatory behaviour, and rudeness. That this man has been specifically chosen to lead the EU team perhaps suggests more about the EU approach to negotiation than anything else, possibly his history of confrontation with the UK – in particular the City of London Financial Sector (Teruel, 2016) – was the reason why he was chosen.

On a final note, it should be clearly understood that the reason behind Barnier's constant pressure on the UK, and his attempts to railroad us into a decision sooner rather than later, is because time is running out. We have just under one year left, by the end of which negotiations must be concluded, and if everything is not agreed by the end of this period, then all that has been agreed so far may be lost – including the 'divorce' payment, which the EU is desperate to have. Mrs May is correct in her choice of tactics, as to delay decisions until the last possible moment, will force Barnier to give concessions; should he not be prepared to do so, then EU-UK trade will have to be conducted along WTO regulations, and that would be disastrous for EU exporters. Thus, Barnier is piling on the pressure to force David Davis's team of UK negotiators to agree to the maintenance of the UK within the SEM and CU – the preferred EU outcome. So forget so-called 'negotiations' with the EU: they will never agree to anything that does not ensure the maintenance of their extravagant lifestyle (they want increasingly more money from us to fund this lifestyle), that will ensure that they can continue to off-load social and economic responsibility for their unemployed onto the UK (the cherished 'freedom of movement'), and will ensure that ultimately they achieve a European 'Superstate' (maintenance of absolute control over the EU structures, finance, diplomacy, law and foreign trade). Such an attitude may well deter other countries (mentioned earlier) from applying for EU membership. The more difficult and unpleasant that the EU makes it for the UK to leave, the more likely other countries will view membership with trepidation.

Now, more than at any time since the late 1930s, we are in danger of giving in to threats and blackmail from a major power in continental Europe. Now, just as then, it is of vital importance to stand up to bullies who issue threats: to 'appease' the EU (pay a large 'divorce' bill, agree on [for us] unfavourable future terms of trade, and allow a degree of freedom of movement, all overseen by the ECJ), would be a capitulation, and a betrayal of what was democratically voted for. As Winston Churchill said, in reference to the UK and another European power which threatened domination and supremacy within continental Europe: "No nation playing the part we play and aspire to play in the world has a right to be in a position where it can be blackmailed (Churchill, 1948:89).

There is nothing really to talk about, and consequently the UK government should threaten to do what the EU fears most – leave without any agreement – a 'hard Brexit'. The EU must be told that, come 29th March 2019, we are leaving – whether we have come to any arrangements or not; we have said we are leaving, and we will leave – preferably without having come to an agreement that ties to the EU for decades, and/or which costs us billions of pounds to secure our freedom. The EU attitude is reminiscent of the song *Hotel California* by The Eagles: "You can check out any time you want, but you can never leave." A 'hard' Brexit is the preferable mode of departure, leaving us without future obligations and commitments. If we threaten to leave without an agreement, EU exporters will very soon bring Juncker, Barnier, and Tusk to their senses: the government must not lose its nerve and succumb to threats, blackmail, and bullying. Following our departure, we will be free to develop bilateral trading and cultural links with whichever countries we choose, and the likelihood is that some of these may well include current EU members, that emboldened by the British example, have sought their own 'exit.'

In the final analysis, if the UK government does not abide by the results of the most important referendum since 1975, and take us irrevocably and immediately out of the EU by 29th March 2019, whilst at the same time ensuring that we do not have to pay billions in what is effectively EU blackmail, then democracy is lost. To hold the government accountable to the will of the people is surely the essence of democracy?

Further Reading and References

Further Reading

Booker, Christopher and North, Richard (2003) *The Great Deception: The Secret History of the European Union*. Continuum, London.

Redwood, John (1997) *Our Currency, Our Country: The Dangers of European Monetary Union*. Penguin Books Ltd., Harmondsworth, Middlesex.

Thatcher, Margaret (2002) *On Europe*. William Collins, London.

References

Ahmed, Kamal (2016) "IMF: EU exit could cause severe damage." BBC Business (12th April); http://www.bbc.co.uk/news/business-36024492

Alexander, Harriet, Nick Squires, and James Badcock (2015) "Austria makes plea over refugee burden as thousands board trains to Vienna." *The Daily Telegraph* (1st September), pp. 12-13

Amaro, Silvia (2018) "Here's how important the UK is to the European Union." CNBC (27th March); https://www.cnbc.com/2017/03/27/european-union-uk-important-brexit.html

Armitstead, Louise (2014) "IMF accepts it was wrong on George Osborne's austerity." *The Telegraph* (6th June); http://www.telegraph.co.uk/finance/economics/10881540/IMF-accepts-it-was-wrong-on-George-Osbornes-austerity.html

Arnold, Martin, Alan Beattie, and Jean Eaglesham (2005) "Sarkozy's 'fool's bargain' tirade deepens French rift with Brussels." *Financial Times* (21st October); https://www.ft.com/content/65e24f4e-41cf-11da-a45d-00000e2511c8

Austin, Henry (2015) "Five of world's biggest investment banks pay no UK corporation tax." *The Independent* (23rd December); http://www.independent.co.uk/news/business/news/five-of-worlds-biggest-investment-banks-pay-no-uk-corporation-tax-a6783716.html

Banks, Martin and Foster, Peter (2016) "Europe forges ahead with plans for 'EU army.'" *The Telegraph* (6th September); http://www.telegraph.co.uk/news/2016/09/06/europe-forges-ahead-with-plans-for-eu-army/

Barber, Tony (2012) "Stretched at the seams." *Financial Times* (9th November); https://www.ft.com/content/c1781c92-281a-11e2-ac7f-00144feabdc0

Barker, Alex and Robinson, Duncan (2016) "UK faces Brexit bill of up to €60bn as Brussels toughens stance." *Financial Times* (15th November); https://www.ft.com/content/480b4ae0-aa9e-11e6-9cb3-bb8207902122

Barker, Alex, Jim Brunsden, and Duncan Robinson (2017) "Brussels pushes to secure lifetime EU rights for migrant workers in Britain." *Financial Times* (21st April), p. 1

Barker, Alex and Byrne, Andrew (2017) "Brussels prepares to sue refugee quota holdouts." *Financial Times* (27th July), p. 6

Barrett, David (2013) "Calls to boycott 'toxic' human rights court." *The Telegraph* (9th July); http://www.telegraph.co.uk/news/uknews/law-and-order/10170325/Calls-grow-to-boycott-toxic-human-rights-court.html

Barrett, David (2015) "British police force at the frontline of Calais crisis sees 35% increase in illegal immigrant arrests." *The Telegraph* (5th August); http://www.telegraph.co.uk/news/uknews/immigration/11784930/British-police-force-at-frontline-of-Calais-crisis-sees-35-increase-in-illegal-immigrant-arrests.html

Barrett, David and Whitehead, Tom (2016) "Hamza daughter-in-law wins European court battle to stay." *The Daily Telegraph* (6th February), p.6

BBC (1973) "1973: Britain Joins the EEC" BBC News (1st January); http://news.bbc.co.uk/onthisday/hi/dates/stories/january/1/newsid_2459000/2459167.stm

BBC (1975) "UK Embraces Europe in Referendum." BBC Home (6th June); http://news.bbc.co.uk/onthisday/hi/dates/stories/june/6/newsid_2499000/2499297.stm

BBC (2011) "Q & A: The Lisbon Treaty." BBC News (17th January); http://news.bbc.co.uk/1/hi/world/europe/6901353.stm

BBC (2012a) "William Hague launches full 'audit' of EU law and the UK." BBC News (12th July); http://www.bbc.co.uk/news/uk-politics-18810566

BBC (2012b) "HSBC to pay $1.9 bn in US money laundering penalties." BBC News (11th December); http://www.bbc.co.uk/news/business-20673466

BBC (2014) "Corruption across EU 'breathtaking' – EU Commission." BBC News (3rd February); http://www.bbc.co.uk/news/world-europe-26014387

BBC (2016a) "IMF: EU exit could cause severe damage." BBC Business News (12th April); http://www.bbc.co.uk/news/business-36024492

BBC (2016b) "Migrant crisis: EU plans penalties for refusing asylum seekers." News (4th May); http://www.bbc.co.uk/news/world-europe-36202490

BBC (2016c) "EU referendum: Kinnock urges young voters to prevent 'Brexit by default.'" BBC News (4th June); http://www.bbc.co.uk/news/uk-politics-eu-referendum-36447926 [p.6]

BBC (2016d) "Eight reasons Leave won the UK's referendum on the EU." BBC News (24th June); http://www.bbc.co.uk/news/uk-politics-eu-referendum-36574526

BBC (2016e) "EU Referendum Results." BBC News (27th June); http://www.bbc.co.uk/news/politics/eu_referendum/results

BBC (2016f) "UK economy grows 0.5% in three months after Brexit vote." BBC Business News (27th October); http://www.bbc.co.uk/news/business-37786467

BBC (2017a) "Tony Blair calls for people to 'rise up' against Brexit." BBC News (17th February); http://www.bbc.co.uk/news/uk-politics-38996179

BBC (2017b) "PM 'must listen, to other parties over Brexit' says Cameron" BBC News (14th June); http://www.bbc.co.uk/news/election-2017-40268504

Beesley, Arthur (2016) "EU-Canada trade deal salvaged after Belgian regions concede." *Financial Times* (27th October); https://www.ft.com/content/1c48cdf6-9c25-11e6-8324-be63473ce146

Bennett, Asa (2017) "Now we know how the Eurocrats will spend our £50 bn Brexit bail-out." *The Daily Telegraph* (10thAugust), p. 4

Bennett, Asa; James Kirkup and Patrick Scott (2017) "The facts behind the £350 m per week EU membership claim." *The Telegraph* (18th September); http://www.telegraph.co.uk/news/0/how-much-do-we-spend-on-the-eu-and-what-else-could-it-pay-for/

Bickerton, Chris (2018) "Brexit is not a one-off, look at Europe's woes." *The Daily Telegraph*, (22nd January), p.16

Birnbaum, Michael (2016) "7 reasons why some Europeans hate the EU" *The Washington Post* (25th June); https://www.washingtonpost.com/news/worldviews/wp/2016/06/25/7-reasons-why-some-europeans-hate-the-eu/?utm_term=.25fa430fb1d8

Blitz, James and Donnan, Shawn (2016) "Fox opens talks over future in WTO." *Financial Times* (8th December), p.2

Boffey, Daniel (2017a) "Denmark to contest UK efforts to 'take back control' of fisheries" *The Guardian* (18th April); https://www.theguardian.com/politics/2017/apr/18/denmark-to-contest-uk-efforts-to-take-back-control-of-fisheries

Boffey, Daniel (2017b) "Juncker says EU will 'move on' from Brexit in state of union speech." The Guardian (13th September); https://www.theguardian.com/politics/2017/sep/13/jean-claude-juncker-plays-down-brexit-in-eu-state-of-union-speech

Boffey, Daniel and Rankin, Jennifer (2017) "UK will rejoin the EU one day, suggests Jean-Claude Juncker." *The Guardian* (19th March); https://www.theguardian.com/world/2017/mar/10/jean-claude-juncer-uk-rejoin-eu-one-day-brexit

Bogdanor, Vernon (2017) "A second Brexit referendum? It's looking more likely by the day." *The Guardian* (3rd August); https://www.theguardian.com/commentisfree/2017/aug/03/second-brexit-referendum-case-getting-stronger-political-deadlock-life-raft#img-1

Booker, Christopher (2015) "Enoch Powell and Tony Benn were right on Europe – it was a great deception." *The Telegraph* (13th June); http://www.telegraph.co.uk/comment/11673377/Enoch-Powell-and-Tony-Benn-were-right-on-Europe-it-was-a-great-deception.html

Booker, Christopher and North, Richard (2003) *The Great Deception: The Secret History of the European Union*. Continuum, London.

Boston, William (2016) "BMW: No immediate impact in U.K. from Brexit vote." *Market Watch* (24th June); http://www.marketwatch.com/story/bmw-no-immediate-impact-in-uk-from-brexit-vote-2016-06-24

Braw, Elisabeth (2017) "Germany is Quietly Building a European Army Under its Command." *Foreign Policy*, D.C. (22ndMay); http://foreignpolicy.com/2017/05/22/germany-is-quietly-building-a-european-army-under-its-command/

Brignall, Miles and Tims, Anna (2015) "EasyJet – the airline that's difficult to deal with." *The Guardian* (5th December); https://www.theguardian.com/business/2015/dec/05/easyjet-complaints-compensation-claims-denied

BSA (2016) *British Social Attitudes 34 (Immigration)*. NatCen Social Research, http://www.bsa.natcen.ac.uk/media/39148/bsa34_immigration_final.pdf

BSF (2016) "Common Fisheries Policy (CFP)" *British Sea Fishing.co.uk* (June); http://britishseafishing.co.uk/conservation/common-fisheries-policy-cfp/

Bulman, May and Fenton, Siobhan (2016) "Brexit: UK immigration controls may shift to Ireland after EU withdrawal." *Independent* (10th October); http://www.independent.co.uk/news/uk/home-news/brexit-ireland-northern-ireland-border-immigration-controls-north-south-peace-process-a7353261.html

Burke, Michael (2013) "If the IMF is criticising UK austerity, things must be bad" *The Guardian* (17thApril); https://www.theguardian.com/

commentisfree/2013/apr/17/imf-criticism-uk-austerity-things-bad

Burton, James and Salmon, James (2017) "US is the UK's top trade partner – NOT the EU after figures show Britain has a surplus of almost £40 billion." *Mailonline* (22nd February); http:www.dailymail.co.uk/news/article-4247434/US-UK-s-trade-partner-NOT-EU.

Byrne, Andrew (2016) "Refugee poll set to bolster Orban." *Financial Times* (30th September), p.6

CAP (2017) "CAP post-2013: Key Graphs & Figures." *CAP Expenditure in the Total EU Expenditure, DG Agriculture and Rural Development, Agricultural Policy Analysis and Perspectives Unit* (March); https://ec.europa.eu/agriculture/sites/agriculture/files/cap-post-2013/graphs/graph1_en.pdf

Carter, Will (2016) "A Guide to Europe's key Eurosceptic parties, and How Successful they are. Who's who in the anti-EU political movements on the continent?" *New Statesman* (4th August); http://www.newstatesman.com/politics/brexit/2016/08/guide-europe-s-key-eurosceptic-parties-and-how-successful-they-are

Cavendish, Camilla (2015) "Britain and Europe must slam the brakes on mass immigration." *The Sunday Times* (8th March), p. 27

Cecchini, Paolo (1992) *1992: The European Challenge.* Wildwood House, Aldershot. ISBN-100704506130

Chaffin, Joshua (2013) "United by hostility." *Financial Times* (16th October); https://www.ft.com/content/ad0d6aee-31ad-11e3-817c-00144feab7de

Chan, Szu Ping (2014) "EU budget: what you need to know." *The Telegraph* (14th November); http://www.telegraph.co.uk/finance/financialcrisis/11221427/EU-budget-what-you-need-to-know.html

Chan, Szu Ping (2016a) "Brexit would raise cost of mortgages, says Osborne." *The Daily Telegraph* (16th April), p. 31

Chan, Szu Ping (2016b) "Brexit can only be bad for UK, says Lagarde." *The Daily Telegraph* (14th May), p.39

Chan, Szu Ping (2016c) "IMF: Brexit will bring eurozone 'years of pain.'" *The Daily Telegraph* (9th July), p.35

Chan, Szu Ping (2016d) " Nestlé boss: we are in the UK 'forever', Brexit doesn't change that." *The Telegraph* (7th August); http://www.telegraph.co.uk/business/2016/08/07/nestl-boss-we-are-in-the-uk-forever-brexit-doesnt-change-that/

Chan, Szu Ping (2016e) "What the UK's fishing industry wants from Brexit."

The Telegraph (1st October); http://www.telegraph.co.uk/business/2016/10/01/ what-the-uks-fishing-industry-wants-from-brexit

Charlemagne (2010) "Are Eurocrats in it for the money?" *The Economist* (22nd June); http://www.economist.com/blogs/charlemagne/2010/06/bureaucrats_ brussels

Chassany, Anne-Sylvaine and Alex Barker (2016) "Leaders see exit pain as Eurosceptic deterrent." *Financial Times* (30th June), p. 5

Chazan, Guy (2016) "Schäuble warns against deeper EU integration." *Financial Times* (11th June), p.8

Chazan, David and Rothwell, James (2016) "Calais protests: lorry drivers begin blocking roads amid anger over violent tactics of migrants trying to reach." *The Telegraph* (5th September); http://www.telegraph.co.uk/news/2016/09/04/ calais-migrants-urged-to-stay-in-jungle-during-port-blockade/

Christafis, Angelique (2017) "Emmanuel Macron vows unity after winning French presidential election." *The Guardian* (8th May); https://www. theguardian.com/world/2017/may/07/emmanuel-macron-wins-french-presidency-marine-le-pen

Churchill, Winston S. (1948) *The Second World War: (Volume 1) The Gathering Storm.* Cassell & Co. Ltd., London.

Clarke, Kenneth (2014) "Kenneth Clarke: Britain ignited the bonfire of Brussels' bureaucracy. We must stay to finish the job." *The Telegraph* (22nd May); http://www.telegraph.co.uk/news/worldnews/europe/eu/10850658/ Britain-ignited-the-bonfire-of-Brussels-bureaucracy.-We-must-stay-to-finish-the-job.html

Clark, Ross and Grimston, Jack (2012) "How to create EU-Topia." *The Sunday Times* (25th November); http://www.thesundaytimes.co.uk/sto/news/focus/ article1167676.ece

Clarke – Billings, Lucy (2015) "Polish rapist who used fake ID to enter Britain is jailed." *The Daily Telegraph* (5th December), p. 11

Cleppe, Pieter (2017) "Juncker has "four or five scenarios" in mind for EU integration after Brexit." Open Europe (28th February); http://openeurope.org. uk/today/blog/juncker-has-four-or-five-scenarios-in-mind-for-eu-integration-after-brexit/

Corbett, Richard (2016) "Salary and Expenses." Http://www.richardcorbett. org. uk/transparency/salary-expenses/

Cowie, Ian (2016) "Voting 'remain' could be our finest hour." *The Sunday Times*

(24th April), p.3

Crisp, James (2017) "Stop 12 pc tax perk for MEPs and staff, Brussels told." *The Daily Telegraph* (11th August), p.8

Crisp, James, and Maidment, Jack (2017) "Pay up if you want free trade deal, says Barnier." *The Daily Telegraph* (22nd September). p.6

Crisp, James, Peter Foster, Gordon Rayner, and Ben Farmer (2017) "Britain's fury at 'unhelpful Barnier.'" *The Daily Telegraph* (29th August). p.1

Croft, Jane (2016) "Ex-Barclays trio guilty of plotting to rig Libor rate." *Financial Times* (5th July), p.17

Darvas, Zsolt, Konstantinos Efstathiou and Inés Goncalves Raposo (2017) "Divorce Settlement or Leaving the Club? A Breakdown of the Brexit Bill."Working Paper (Issue 03), pp. 1-57, Bruegel, Brussels.

Davies, Gareth (2016) "Panicked EU chiefs hurriedly invite Trump to discuss trade negotiations over fears America's new president would rather deal with BRITAIN." *Mailonline* (9th November); http://www.dailymail.co.uk/news/article-3921012/Panicked-EU-chiefs-hurriedly-invite-Trump-discuss-trade-negotiations-fears-America-s-new-president-deal-BRITAIN.html

Day, Matthew and Foster, Peter (2015) "Any new benefit limits in UK must apply to British too, warn Czechs." *The Daily Telegraph* (4th December), p.19

Day, Matthew and Waterfield, Bruno (2014b) "Britain's £10 m benefits bill for migrants who go home." *The Daily Telegraph* (27th September), p. 8

Delhey, Jan (2007) "Do Enlargements Make the European Union Less Cohesive? An Analysis of Trust Between EU Nationalities." *Journal of Common Market Studies*, Vol.45 (2), pp. 253-279

Dinmore, Guy (2013) "Finnish PM softens bailout stance as euroscepticism grows." *Financial Times* (16th October); https://www.pressreader.com/china/financial-times-asia/20131016/281621008064236

Dominiczak, Peter (2014a) "Tony Blair helped to double Britain's EU payments." *The Telegraph* (30th October); http://www.telegraph.co.uk/news/worldnews/europe/eu/11200124/Tony-Blair-helped-to-double-Britains-EU-payments.html

Dominiczak, Peter (2014b) "EU 'must give way to UK on migrants.'" *The Daily Telegraph* (15th November), p.1

Dominiczak, Peter (2015) "Migration 'harming society.'" *The Daily Telegraph* (10th October), p.1

Dominiczak, Peter and Holehouse, Matthew (2016) "PM demands EU migrant deal." *The Daily Telegraph* (29th June), p.1

Dominiczak, Peter and Swinford, Steven (2016) "Goldman Sachs donates six – figure sum to pro-Europe campaign." *The Daily Telegraph* (21st January), p.4

Dominiczak, Peter and Waterfield, Bruno (2014) "Eurocrats dismiss Tory plan for Bill of Rights." *The Daily Telegraph* (4th October), p.2

Donnellan, Aimee (2016) "Hard Brexit to cost 2,000 Goldman jobs." *The Sunday Times* (9th October), p. B1

Doyle, Jack and Warren, Lydia (2011) "Nigerian rapist who can't be deported because European judges say it would violate his right to family life." *Mailonline* (20th September); http://www.dailymail.co.uk/news/article-2039702/UK-deport-Nigerian-rapist-violate-right-family-life.html

Dowling, Kevin (2015) "Migrants spark holiday chaos." *The Sunday Times* (26th July), p.6

Duke, Simon and Smith, David (2017) "'Even-money chance' Britain tips into recession, warn economists." *The Sunday Times* (23rd July), p. 2

Editorial (2016a) "Migrants to the West must obey the rules." *The Daily Telegraph* (9th January), p.21

Editorial (2016b) "The EU shows why it needs to be reformed." *The Daily Telegraph* (20th February), p. 23

Editorial (2016c) "The EU bureaucrats cannot cope with democracy." *The Telegraph* (27th May); http://www.telegraph.co.uk/opinion/2016/05/27/the-eu-bureaucrats-cannot-cope-with-democracy

Editorial (2016d) " 20 reasons you should vote to leave the European Union." *The Telegraph* (22nd June); http://www.telegraph.co.uk/news/2016/06/22/20-reasons-you-should-vote-to-leave-the-european-union/

Editorial (2016e) "Mr Juncker's power must be curtailed." *The Daily Telegraph* (29th June), p. 19

Editorial (2016f) "A distrusted man who inspired Brexit." *The Daily Telegraph* (29th October), p. 25

Editorial (2017a) "Make our aid budget work for Brexit." *The Sunday Times* (19th February), p. 20

Editorial (2017b) "The bullying EU." *The Daily Telegraph* (29th April), p.19

Editorial (2017c) "A phoney war over Brexit and the British economy." *Financial Times* (27th July), p. 10

Editorial (2017d) "EC Expenses jamboree rot starts at the top." *The Daily*

Telegraph (10th August), p. 15

Editorial (2017e) "Focus on our strengths, not negotiation tactics." *The Daily Telegraph* (1st September), p. 17

EEAS (2016) http://eeas.europa.eu/delegations/index_en.htm .

Efstathiou, Zoe (2016) "Fury as EU officials handed £15M PAY RISE as Brussels continues tirade on national debts" *Express* (28th November); http://www.express.co.uk/news/world/737149/Brussels-Nigel-farage-pay-rise-Jean-Claude-juncker-salary-EU-ukip

Elgot, Jessica, Larry Elliott, and Nicola Davis (2016) "Treasury to guarantee post-Brexit funding for EU-backed projects." *The Guardian* (13th August); https://www.theguardian.com/politics/2016/aug/13/philip-hammond-treasury-to-guarantee-post-brexit-funding-for-eu-backed-projects

Elliott , Larry (2016) "UK trade deficit with EU hits new record" *The Guardian* (10th May); http://www.theguardian.com/business/2016/may/10/uk-trade-deficit-hits-new-record-of-24bn-pounds-eu-referendum-brexit

Erixon, Fredrick (2017) "Britain and the EU probably will reach a trade deal. Here's why." *The Spectator* (1st April); https://www.spectator.co.uk/2017/04/britain-and-the-eu-probably-will-reach-a-trade-deal-heres-why/

EU Budget (2017) "Where does the money come from?" *European Commission* (15th February); http://ec.europa.eu/budget/explained/budg_system/financing/fin_en.cfm

EUobserver (2014) "EU students fail to repay UK loans." *EUobserver* (24th June); https://EUobserver.com/tickers/124714

Eurobarometer (2013) Standard Eurobarometer 79: "Public Opinion in the European Union. Directorate-General for Communication" (DG COMM "Research and Speechwriting" Unit), Brussels. Also available at: http://ec.europa.eu.public_opinion/index_en.html

EUROSTAT (2017) "Youth Unemployment Figures" (3rd July); http://ec.europa.eu/eurostat/statisticsexplained/index.php/File:Youth_unemployment_figures,_2007-2016_(%25)_T1.png

Farand, Chloe (2016) "Six British multinationals 'did not pay any UK corporation tax in 2014'" *The Independent* (31st January); http://www.independent.co.uk/news/uk/six-british-multinationals-including-shell-vodafone-lloyds-banking-group-did-not-paid-any-a6844676.html

Fildes, Nic (2017) "Telefónica states commitment to stay in Britain." *Financial Times* (28th June), p.20

Filkins, Dexter (2017) "Turkey's Vote Makes Erdoğan Effectively a Dictator."

The New Yorker (17th April); http://www.newyorker.com/news/news-desk/turkeys-vote-makes-erdogan-effectively-a-dictator

Flood, Chris (2016) "EU regulator warns Brexit is a threat to UK funds." *Financial Times* (27th May); http://financial-times-yahoopartner.tumblr.com/post/144998113889/eu-regulator-warns-brexit-is-a-threat-to-uk

Foster, Peter (2016) "EU deal: What David Cameron asked for ... and what he actually got." *The Telegraph* (14th June); http://www.telegraph.co.uk/news/2016/05/19/eu-deal-what-david-cameron-asked-for-and-what-he-actually-got/

Foster, Peter (2017) "EU to reject parallel talks on trade and divorce deal." *The Daily Telegraph* (31st March), p.9

Foster, Peter and Day, Matthew (2016) "EU 'must stand firm against UK demands.'" *The Daily Telegraph* (8th October), p 18

Foster, Peter and Holehouse, Matthew (2015) "Merkel 'expects Cameron to back EU army' in exchange for renegotiation" *The Telegraph* (12th September); http://www.telegraph.co.uk/news/worldnews/europe/eu/11861247/Merkel-expects-Cameron-to-back-EU-army-in-exchange-for-renegotiation.html

Foster, Peter, Justin Huggler, and Richard Orange (2016) "Migrant sex attacks backlash." *The Daily Telegraph* (9th January), p.1

Fraser, Isabelle (2016) "What does Brexit mean for house prices? If we leave will it solve the housing crisis?" *The Telegraph* (20th June); http://www.telegraph.co.uk/property/house-prices/what-does-brexit-mean-for-house-prices-if-we-leave-will-it-solve/

Fredenburgh, Jez and Hart, Tom (2016) "Lord Plumb and Kendall unequivocal on EU referendum." *Farmers Weekly* (24th February); http://www.fwi.co.uk/news/video-lord-plumb-and-kendall-unequivocal-on-eu-referendum.htm

FT Reporters (2015) "Investors and expats face the risks from a possible Grexit." *Financial Times* (4th July), p.4

Ganesh, Janan (2014) "Resentment of migrants is about feelings not facts." *Financial Times* (4th March), p.6

Garcia-Herrero, Alicia and Xu, Jianwei (2016) "What Consequences would a Post-Brexit China-UK Trade Deal Have for the EU?" *Policy Contribution* (Issue No. 18), Bruegel.org; http://bruegel.org/2016/10/what-consequences-would-a-post-brexit-china-uk-trade-deal-have-for-the-eu/

Geier, Jens (2016) EU budget: "We have to deal with the problem caused by Brexit." *EU Affairs*. (26th October); http://www.europarl.europa.eu/news/en/headlines/priorities/20161116TST51301/20161014STO47383/eu-budget-we-have-to-deal-with-the-problem-caused-by-brexit

Gillespie, James (2011) "Landlocked countries get EU fishing money." *The Sunday Times* (2nd October); https://www.thetimes.co.uk/article/landlocked-countries-get-eu-fishing-money-2b2qk93ssrh

Giles, Chris and Waldmeir (2016) "Osborne presses global finance ministers to warn against Brexit." *Financial Times* (26th February), p.1

Giugliano, Ferdinando (2015) *Financial Times* (2nd June); https://www.ft.com/content/1fd77e84-0920-11e5-b643-00144feabdc0

Glapinski, Adam (2017) "Deeper European integration is on hold indefinitely." *Financial Times* (30th May); https://www.ft.com/content/37144902-448c-11e7-8d27-59b4dd6296b8

Gorton, Matthew, Sophia Davidova, and Tomas Ratinger (2000) "The Competitiveness of Agriculture in Bulgaria and the Czech Republic *Vis-à-Vis* the European Union (CEEC and EU Agricultural Competitiveness)." *Comparative Economic Studies*, Vol. 42 (1), pp. 59-86

Goulard, Sylvie (2016) "After Brexit, further integration is needed to save the EU." *Financial Times* (7th November); https://www.ft.com/content/58c47ba4-a1ed-11e6-aa83-bcb58d1d2193

Gray, Jasmine (2017) "Here's What Jeremy Corbyn Actually Said About Student Debt Ahead Of The General Election." *Huffpost United Kingdom* (24th July); http://www.huffingtonpost.co.uk/entry/jeremy-corbyn-student-debt-general-election_uk_5975a97de4b09e5f6cd0619c

Grew, Tony and Hookham, Mark (2012) "Taxpayer's millions fuel Ford Transit move to Turkey." *The Sunday Times* (4th November); http://www.thesundaytimes.co.uk/sto/news/uk_news/National/article1159026.ece

Grew, Tony and Pancevski, Bojan (2017) "Keir Starmer makes Labour 'soft Brexit' party." *The Times* (27th August); https://www.thetimes.co.uk/article/keir-starmer-makes-labour-soft-brexit-party-cmrxvbnkv

Grice, Andrew (2016) "Philip Hammond pledges billions of pounds funding to organisations to plug post-Brexit shortfall." *Independent* (12th August); http://www.independent.co.uk/news/uk/politics/philip-hammond-pledges-billions-of-pounds-funding-to-organisations-to-plug-post-brexit-shortfall-a7188201.html

Grimston, Jack (2012) "Britain's EU bill rises by £270 m." *The Sunday Times* (4th November); http://www.thesundaytimes.co.uk/sto/news/Politics/article1159028.ece

Gutteridge, Nick (2016a) "Night of terror: Calais migrant thugs attack car and set fire to road to stop truckers." *Express* (10th April); http://www.express.co.uk/news/world/659643/Calais-migrants-refugees-Jungle-attack-violence-car-barricade-road-UK-truckers

Gutteridge, Nick (2016b) "'Not worth it anymore!' HAMMER BLOW for Juncker as nations dump EU trade deals post-Brexit." *The Express* (22nd September); http://www.express.co.uk/news/world/713260/European-Union-EU-trade-Africa-Caribbean-Pacific-EPAs-TTIP-CETA-Brexit

Habermas, Jurgen, Peter Bofinger, Julian and Nida-Rűmelin (2012) "Only deeper European unification can save the eurozone." *The Guardian* (9th August); https://www.theguardian.com/commentisfree/2012/aug/09/deeper-european-unification-save-eurozone

Hall, Melanie and Holehouse, Matthew (2015) "Germany wants mandatory quotas to deal with refugees." *The Daily Telegraph* (19th September), p. 18

Hannah Kuchler, Kate A. and Rigby, Elizabeth (2013) "Immigration surge threatens to fuel Conservative tensions." *Financial Times* (31st January), p.5

Hannan, Daniel (2016) "Those of us who voted Leave are democrats – not racists." *The Daily Telegraph* (29th June), p.18

Harris, Tom (2017) "Tony Blair and Peter Mandelson ignore the lessons of history on Brexit." *The Telegraph* (20th February); http://www.telegraph.co.uk/opinion/2017/02/20/tony-blair-peter-mandelson-ignore-lessons-history-brexit/

Heath, Allister (2016) " Why banks won't leave if we vote for Brexit." *The Telegraph (Business),* (3rd June); http://www.telegraph.co.uk/business/2016/06/03/why-banks-wont-leave-if-we-vote-for-brexit/

Heath, Allister (2017) "Brussels' mad attempt to force us to pay reparations will backfire badly." *The Daily Telegraph* (4thMay), p. 18

Henley, Jon and Roberts, Dan (2016) "Reality check: will it take 10 years to do a UK-EU trade deal post Brexit?" *The Guardian* (15th December); https://www.theguardian.com/politics/2016/dec/15/reality-check-will-it-take-10-years-to-do-a-uk-eu-trade-deal-post-brexit

Hennessy, Patrick (2012) "No shadow cabinet return for Tony Blair." *The Telegraph* (4th August); http://www.telegraph.co.uk/news/politics/tony-blair/9451537/No-shadow-cabinet-return-for-Tony-Blair.html

Hill, Jenny (2017) "Migrant crisis: Germany sees massive drop in asylum seekers." *BBC News* (11th January); http://www.bbc.co.uk/news/world-europe-38584705

Holehouse, Matthew (2015a) "Cameron flags up benefits of EU." *The Daily Telegraph* (20th October), p.4

Holehouse, Matthew (2015b) "Visit a military cemetery for a reminder of the dangers of Brexit, says Juncker." *The Daily Telegraph* (5th March), p.13

Holehouse, Matthew (2015c) "EU to fork out £2m, just for a dinner service." *The Daily Telegraph* (18th July), p.4

Holehouse, Matthew (2015d) "Fraud allegations and waste as EU hands out money faster than states can spend it." *The Telegraph* (10th November); http://www.telegraph.co.uk/news/worldnews/europe/eu/11985763/Fraud-allegations-and-waste-as-EU-hands-out-money-faster-than-states-can-spend-it.html

Holehouse, Matthew (2016a) "New Year's Eve attacks nothing to do with immigration, says EU." *The Daily Telegraph* (30th January), p.6

Holehouse, Matthew (2016b) "EU pays MEPs £40,000 a year in expenses, no receipts needed." *The Daily Telegraph* (2nd April), p.15

Hollinger, Peggy (2017)"Rolls-Royce workers hail £150 million investment." *Financial Times* (30th June), p.18

Hope, Christopher (2012) "I want to lead Europe (but not now), says Tony Blair." *The Telegraph* (17th June); http://www.telegraph.co.uk/news/politics/tony-blair/9337358/I-want-to-lead-Europe-but-not-now-says-Tony-Blair.html

Hope, Christopher (2014) "Parts of Britain are foreign land, says Farage." *The Daily Telegraph* (1stMarch), p. 6

Hope, Christopher (2016) "Don't label us racist for raising voter's concerns on immigration, says Patel." *The Daily Telegraph* (16thApril), pp. 14-15

Hope, Christopher (2017) "Britain to be bound by European human rights laws for at least another five years even if Tories win election." *The Telegraph* (18th May); http://www.telegraph.co.uk/news/2017/05/18/britain-bound-european-human-rights-laws-least-another-five/

Hope, Christopher and Barrett, David (2016) "NI numbers that only last a year 'will keep track of migrants'." *The Daily Telegraph* (14th May), p. 9

Hope, Christopher and Johnson, Simon (2017) "Cable holds talks with Tory MPs to frustrate Brexit." *The Daily Telegraph*(23rd June), p. 9

Howard, Michael and Aikens, Richard (2016) "The EU's court is picking apart our laws." *The Telegraph* (22nd June); http://www.telegraph.co.uk/news/2016/06/22/the-eus-court-is-picking-apart-our-laws/

Huggler, Justin (2015) "Bavaria threatens to turn back migrants at border in direct challenge to chancellor." *The Daily Telegraph* (10th October), p. 6

Huggler, Justin (2016) "We have lost track of 130,000 asylum seekers, admit

German authorities." *The Daily Telegraph* (27th February), p. 9

Hughes, Laura (2016a) "Sir Bernard Ingham: EU is corrupt, useless and riddled with fraud." *The Telegraph* (27th January); http://www.telegraph.co.uk/news/newstopics/eureferendum/12124910/Sir-Bernard-Ingham-EU-is-corrupt-useless-and-riddled-with-fraud.html

Hughes, Laura (2016c) "Prospect of early general election increases after High Court rules Government cannot trigger Article 50 without parliamentary approval." *The Telegraph* (3rd November); http://www.telegraph.co.uk/news/2016/11/03/high-court-to-rule-on-brexit-legal-battle-and-theresa-mays-decis/

Hughes, Laura and Swinford, Steven (2016) "Bavarian MP presses for new business links with Britain." *The Daily Telegraph* (26th November), p.8

Jenkins, Simon (2016) "Brexit could cause war? Utter nonsense, David Cameron." *The Guardian* (9th May); https://www.theguardian.com/commentisfree/2016/may/09/brexit-cause-war-nonsense-david-cameron-history-eu-debate

Johnson, Simon (2016) "Price of meat could rise as farmers pass on tariff costs to shoppers, PM suggests." *The Daily Telegraph* (6th March), p. 11

Johnston, Ian (2016a) "EU referendum: BMW warns staff in UK Rolls Royce factories of Brexit risks." *Independent* (2nd March); http://www.independent.co.uk/news/world/europe/eu-referendum-bmw-warns-staff-at-uk-companies-owned-by-german-car-giant-of-brexit-risks-a6908676.html

Johnston, Philip (2016b) "Immigration is key to the EU vote, so will Boris change his tune?" *The Daily Telegraph* (24th February), p. 20

Johnston, Philip (2017) "Germany has shown that it's going to play dirty in the Brexit Games." *The Daily Telegraph* (3rd May), p. 14

Jones, Sam and Robinson, Duncan (2014) "Jihadis slip through Europe's porous borders." *Financial Times* (4th November), p.7

Kelley, Ben (2016) "Anna Soubry is wrong. Immigration has to be a red line in our Brexit negotiations." *The Telegraph* (31st August); http://www.telegraph.co.uk/news/2016/08/31/brexit-will-give-britain-back-control-of-its-destiny-it-must-not/

Kentish, Ben (2017) "Donald Trump says he previously claimed Nato was 'obsolete' because he 'did not know much about it." *The Independent* (26th April); http://www.independent.co.uk/news/world/americas/us-politics/donald-trump-not-know-much-nato-alliance-wolf-blitzer-cnn-obsolete-a7702201.html

Keunssberg, Laura (2016) "How long will post-Brexit trade deal take?" *BBC*

News (Politics) (15th December); available at: http://www.bbc.co.uk/news/uk-politics-38319344

Khan, Mehreen (2015) "Euro stumbles towards its goal of closer union." *The Daily Telegraph* (24th October), p.41

Khan, Shehab (2016) "European Parliament backs plans to create a defence union." *The Independent* (22nd November); http://www.independent.co.uk/news/world/europe/european-parliament-nato-backs-plans-create-defence-union-a7432706.html

Kinchen, Rosie (2018) "Lord remain is here to coax us back to Brussels." *The Sunday Times* (7th January), p. 29

Kirkup, James (2008) "Peter Mandelson can claim £1 million in European Union pay-off and pension." *The Telegraph* (12 October); http://www.telegraph.co.uk/news/politics/labour/3183375/Peter-Mandelson-can-claim-1-million-in-European-Union-pay-off-and-pension.html

Klaus, Václav (2007) "The Future of the EU – Where do we go Now?" *The European Journal,* Vol. 14 (1), p.5

Kleinman, Mark (2014) "Nestlé Chair warns over UK exit from Europe." *Sky News* (24th January);http://news.sky.com/story/nestl233-chair-warns-over-uk-exit-from-europe-10420127

Lamont, Norman (1994) "Europe: this far and no further: Opt-outs will not save us from federalism, argues Norman Lamont. The 'party of the nation' must guarantee Britain's right to stand alone." *Independent* (11th October); http://www.independent.co.uk/voices/europe-this-far-and-no-further-opt-outs-will-not-save-us-from-federalism-argues-norman-lamont-the-1442493.html

Lawson, Dominic (2011) "Ridley was right." *The Spectator* (24th September); https://www.spectator.co.uk/2011/09/ridley-was-right/

Lawson, Dominic (2016a) "Pass the bourbon and I'll pour you a hard shot of truth about the EU." *The Sunday Times* (28th February), p. 20

Lawson, Dominic (2016b) "The queue outside the doctor's that leads all the way out of the EU." *The Sunday Times* (12th June), p. 20

Lawson, Dominic (2017) "A reminder for remainers: 'the uneducated' protect us from brilliant idiots." *The Sunday Times* (12th February), p. 20

Leppard, David (2012) "British betrayed by EU extradition laws." *The Sunday Times* (4th November); https://www.thetimes.co.uk/article/british-betrayed-by-eu-extradition-laws-ph8rzsdmp2g

Levy, Mickey (2012) "Competitiveness among EU nations: Constraining wages is the key." *VoxEU.org* (19th January); http://voxeu.org/article/how-restore-competitiveness-eu

Liberal Democrats (2010) *Liberal Democrat Manifesto 2010: Change That Works for You.* Chris Fox, London. ISBN: 1-907046-19-3; also available at: http://www.politicsresources.net/area/uk/ge10/man/parties/libdem_manifesto_2010.pdf

Lilico, Andrew (2014) "After 2020, all EU members will have to adopt the euro." *The Telegraph*(1stJuly); http://www.telegraph.co.uk/finance/economics/10935617/After-2020-all-EU-members-will-have-to-adopt-the-euro.html

Lilley, Peter (2016) "The truth about Britain's trade outside the European Union" *The Telegraph* (26thMay); http://www.telegraph.co.uk/news/2016/05/26/the-truth-about-britains-trade-outside-the-european-union/

Loizou, Kiki, John Collingridge, and Laura Onita (2015) "Calais chaos: lost cargoes, lost clients and months to fix the mess." *The Sunday Times* (2nd August), p.2

MacAskill, Ewen (2017) "Russia says US troops arriving in Poland pose threat to its security." *The Guardian* (12th January); https://www.theguardian.com/us-news/2017/jan/12/doubts-over-biggest-us-deployment-in-europe-since-cold-war-under-trump

MacLellan, Kylie (2016) "Britain faces long road to post-Brexit trade deals." *Reuters*, London (8th September); http://uk.reuters.com/article/uk-britain-eu-trade-analysis-idUKKCN11D1CR

Maidment, Jack (2018) "Questions over Lord Sainsbury's £3.7 m donations to Remain groups." *The Daily Telegraph* (3rd January), p.4

Mann, Jim (2016) "Britons and Europe: the survey results." *The Guardian* (20th March); https://www.theguardian.com/politics/2016/mar/20/britons-on-europe-survey-results-opinium-poll-referendum

Mann, Michael (2002) "Seeds of change." *Financial Times* (30th January), p.15

Martin, Ben (2017) "HSBC chairman warns of a Brexit 'Jenga tower' of City job losses." *The Daily Telegraph* (11th January), p.3

Marr, Andrew (2017) Interview with Jeremy Corbyn. *The Andrew Marr Show* (23rd July); http://news.bbc.co.uk/1/shared/bsp/hi/pdfs/23071701.pdf (Transcript, pp. 1-9)

Mason, Rowena (2013) "We're not about to stop cutting, says George Osborne after IMF austerity warning." *The Telegraph* (24th January); http://www.telegraph.co.uk/news/politics/9824245/Were-not-about-to-stop-cutting-says-

George-Osborne-after-IMF-austerity-warning.html

Mason, Rowena (2016a) "Gove: EU immigrant influx will make NHS unsustainable by 2030." *The Guardian* (20th May); https://www.theguardian.com/politics/2016/may/20/eu-immigrant-influx-michael-gove-nhs-unsustainable

Mason, Rowena (2016b) "How did UK end up voting to leave the European Union?" *The Guardian* (24th June); https://www.theguardian.com/politics/2016/jun/24/how-did-uk-end-up-voting-leave-european-union

Mason, Rowena (2017) "Tony Blair calls on remainers to 'rise up in defence of our beliefs'." *The Guardian* (16th February); https://www.theguardian.com/politics/2017/feb/16/tony-blair-remainers-rise-up-brexit

Mason, Rowena and Elgot, Jessica (2017) "Tony Blair: debilitated Labour is facilitating a disastrous Brexit." *The Guardian* (17th February); https://www.theguardian.com/politics/2017/feb/17/tony-blair-debilitated-labour-is-facilitating-a-disastrous-brexit

McBride, James (2016) "The World Trade Organization (WTO)." *Council on Foreign Relations,* New York (12th September); https://www.cfr.org/backgrounder/world-trade-organization-wto

McDonald, Henry (2016) "Britain to push post-Brexit UK immigration controls back to Irish border." *The Guardian* (9th October); https://www.theguardian.com/politics/2016/oct/09/britain-to-push-post-brexit-uk-immigration-controls-back-to-irish-border

McFadyen, Siobhan (2017) "The cost of Merkel's refugee crisis: Germany to spend £37 bn to fix migrant crisis." *Express* (31st January); http://www.express.co.uk/news/world/761162/Angela-Merkel-Germany-Migrant-Crisis-costs-refugees

McLean, Paul (2017) "EU fishing fleet urges post-Brexit access to UK seas" *Financial Times* (22nd March); https://www.ft.com/content/958c7e28-0f1c-11e7-b030-768954394623

McNamara, Kathleen R. (2010) "The Eurocrisis and the Uncertain Future of European Integration." *Council for Foreign Relations* (24th September), New York; https://www.cfr.org/report/eurocrisis-and-uncertain-future-european-integration

Mercer, Chris (2016) "Brexit: UK to seek share of EU wine cellar – report." *Decanter* (3rd October); http://www.decanter.com/wine-news/brexit-uk-seek-share-eu-wine-cellar-report-332694/

Midgley, Dominic (2016) "Brussels' faceless bureaucrats REVEALED... and here are their endless perks YOU pay for." *Express* (8th June); http://www.express.co.uk/news/politics/677905/EU-president-tusk-juncker-schulz-pay-perks-pensions-revealed-unelected

Milne, Richard and Spiegel, Peter (2016) "Fraying Union." *Financial Times* (26thFebruary), p.11

Minford, Patrick (2002) "Should Britain Join the Euro? The Chancellor's Five Tests Examined." *Institute of Economic Affairs,* (August, 2002). Publications, London. Also available at: http://www.iea.org.uk/sites/default/files/publications/files/upldbook147pdf.pdf

Moore, Charles (2015) "Britain will accept immigration – but only if it is kept under control." *The Daily Telegraph* (1st August), p. 24

Moore, Charles (2016) "Our bigoted elite have not even considered the case for leaving EU." *The Daily Telegraph* (3rd March), p. 16

Moore, Charles (2017) "Only those who don't want to leave see Brexit as mind-blowingly complicated." *The Daily Telegraph* (7th January), p. 18

Mordasov, Mikhail (2012) "Russia's Influence in Breakaway Territories in the Region." *Strafor/World View* (28th February); https://www.stratfor.com/analysis/russias-influence-breakaway-territories-region

Morley, Katie and Crisp, James (2017) "Shoppers hoover up powerful vacuum cleaners before EU ban." *The Daily Telegraph* (1st September), p.1

Monnet, Jean (1978) *Memoirs.* Collins, London.

Mulholland, Rory and Webb, Oscar (2015) "From east to west, Europe's borders under pressure." *The Sunday Telegraph* (18th October)' pp.18-19

Murray, Douglas (2015) "Euroscepticism is growing all over Europe." *The Spectator* (3rd October); https://www.spectator.co.uk/2015/10/euroscepticism-is-growing-all-over-europe/

Nelson, Fraser (2016) "George Osborn threatens to punish voters with tax rise if they defy him on Brexit." *The Spectator* (14th June); http://blogs.spectator.co.uk/2016/06/george-osborne-threatens-punish-voters-tax-rises-defy-brexit/

Nineham, Chris (2014) "Don't be nostalgic about Tony Blair. His effect on Britain and beyond was toxic." *The Guardian* (14th April); http://www.theguardian.com/commentisfree/2014/apr/14/blairism-britain-iraq-war-tony-blair

Noak, Rick (2016) " 2,000 men 'sexually assaulted 1,200 women' at Cologne New Year's Eve party." *The Independent Online* (11th July); http://www.independent.co.uk/news/world/europe/cologne-new-years-eve-mass-sex-attacks-leaked-document-a7130476.html

Nolan, Dan, Phillipson, Alice and Holehouse, Matthew (2015) "Eastern bloc stands firm against EU quotas." *The Daily Telegraph* (21st September), p. 18

O'Brien, Zoie (2016) "GREAT ESCAPE: Juncker's plan for ALL members to adopt euro revealed just DAYS after Brexit." *Express* (28th June); http://www.express.co.uk/news/world/683883/EU-plans-members-adopt-euro-revealed-DAYS-Brexit-Britain

Oltermann, Philip (2016) "German poll finds one in three firms would leave UK after Brexit." *The Guardian* (14th February); https://www.theguardian.com/politics/2016/feb/14/eu-referendum-poll-1-in-3-firms-leave-uk-brexit

Oliver, Christian, James Fontanella-Khan and Andrew Byrne (2014) "EU divided on response to Russian invasion." *Financial Times* (5th March); https://www.ft.com/content/5e2e348c-a483-11e3-9cb0-00144feab7de

O'Neill, Brendan (2016) "Brexit voters are not thick, not racist: just poor." *The Spectator* (2nd July); https://www.spectator.co.uk/2016/07/brexit-voters-are-not-thick-not-racist-just-poor/

ONS (2015) "UK Trade in Goods Estimates and the 'Rotterdam Effect'" *UK Trade, December 2014*. Office for National Statistics. (February 2015); http://webarchive.nationalarchives.gov.uk/20160105160709/http://www.ons.gov.uk/ons/rel/uktrade/uk-trade/december-2014/index.html

Palmer, Alasdair (2012) "Multiculturalism has left Britain with a toxic legacy." *The Telegraph* (11th February); http://telegraph.co.uk/news/uknews/immigration/9075849/Multiculturalism-has-left-Britain-with-a-toxic-legacy.html

Pancevski, Bojan (2012) "93 days' holiday: the perks of a Eurocrat." *The Sunday Times* (25th November), p.6

Pancevski, Bojan (2015) "Merkel fights to keep door open as German fear of migrants grows." *The Sunday Times* (11th October), p32

Pancevski, Bojan (2016) "Seven Paris attackers slipped into Europe as refugees." *The Sunday Times* (2nd October), p.22

Parker, George and Allen, Kate (2016) "Brexit would hit economy hard, BlackRock warns." *Financial Times* (2nd March), p4

Parker, George, and Pickard, Jim (2016) "Obama gives powerful warning against Brexit." *Financial Times* (22nd April); https://www.ft.com/content/ba4fd8a4-089c-11e6-b6d3-746f8e9cdd33

Payne, Adam (2016) "Britain's immigrants are helping the NHS, not hurting it." *Business Insider* (27th May) [http://uk.businessinsider.com/nhs-analysis-immigration-impact-on-uk-public-services-2016-5]

Pearson, Allison (2016a) "'The risks of staying in are infinitely greater.'" *The Daily Telegraph* (28th May), p.27

Pearson, Allison (2016b) "It's not nice being accused of racism for raising the concerns of ordinary people." *The Daily Telegraph* (4th June), p.16

Pearson, Allison (2016c) "Dyson's hairdryer is at full blast and it's pointing right at EU bureaucrats." *The Daily Telegraph* (11th June), p.13

Peel, Quentin (2016) "Historic misunderstanding underlies UK-EU relationship on Churchill anniversary." *Financial Times* (19th September); https://www.ft.com/content/3d6bbabc-7122-11e6-a0c9-1365ce54b926

Perraudin, Frances and Adams, Richard (2016) "UK student loans: 'we will trace and prosecute borrowers who don't pay.'" *The Guardian* (12th February); https://www.theguardian.com/uk-news/2016/feb/12/student-loans-we-will-trace-prosecute-borrowers-dont-pay

Pickard, Jim (2014) "Ukip finds fertile ground in rundown seaside town." *Financial Times* (9th October), p.2

Pickard, Jim (2017) "Clarke raises possibility of no-deal Brexit veto." *Financial Times* (17th October), p.3

Pickard, Jim and Hollinger, Peggy (2016) "Business faces 'confusion' over post-Brexit regulation, CBI warns." *Financial Times* (21st December); https://www.ft.com/content/7dc9a004-c6c4-11e6-8f29-9445cac8966f

Pickard, Jim, George Parker, and Richard McGregor (2013) "US warns Britain against leaving EU." *Financial Times* (10th January), p.6

Platten, Guy (2017) "The Brexit die has been cast, so let's end the carping." *The Daily Telegraph* (22nd September), p. 2

Politi, James (2017) "'Red' Italy shifts right." *Financial Times* (16th November), p.7

Pop, Valentina (2014) "Who is Jean-Claude Juncker?" *EUobserver* (27th June); https://euobserver.com/eu-elections/124789

Porter, Mark and Poucreau, Ana (2017) "The Russians are coming." *The Sunday Times Magazine* (8th January), pp.19-25.

Protts, Justin (2016) "Will UK financial services suffer from losing passporting rights after Brexit?" *Civitas EU Facts* (6th July); http://www.eu-facts.org.uk/arguments-by-topic/will-uk-financial-services-suffer-from-losing-passporting-rights-after-brexit/

Pugh, Tom (2015) "Two men arrested after walking through Channel Tunnel

from Calais." *The Independent Online* (7th October); http://www.independent.
co.uk/news/uk/crime/two-men-arrested-after-walking-through-channel-
tunnel-from-calais-a6684116.html

Rachman, Gideon (2012a) "Welcome to Berlin, Europe's new capital." *Financial
Times* (22nd October); https://www.ft.com/content/01db45ba-1c32-11e2-a63b-
00144feabdc0

Rankin, Jennifer (2016a) "Is the EU undemocratic?" *The Guardian* (13th June);
https://www.theguardian.com/world/2016/jun/13/is-the-eu-undemocratic-
referendum-reality-check

Rankin, Jennifer (2016b) "Britain must learn from the EU-Canada Ceta
trade deal saga." *The Guardian* (29th October) https://www.theguardian.com/
business/2016/oct/29/britain-must-learn-from-the-eu-canada-ceta-trade-deal-
saga

Rayner, Gordon (2015a) "Cameron warns chaos may last all summer." *The
Daily Telegraph* (1st August), p. 4

Rayner, Gordon (2015b) "Life at a standstill in the Car Park of England." *The
Daily Telegraph* (1st August), p. 4

Rayner, Gordon and Hope, Christopher (2017) "Cut the EU red tape
choking Britain after Brexit to set the country free from the shackles
of Brussels." *The Telegraph* (28th March); http://www.telegraph.co.uk/
news/2017/03/27/cut-eu-red-tape-choking-britain-brexit-set-country-free-
shackles/

Rayner, Gordon, Jack Maidment, and Christoper Hope (2018) "£44m to keep
border at Calais." *The Daily Telegraph* (18th January), p. 1

Rettman, Andrew (2017) "Russian missiles pose new threat to Europe."
Euobserver (9th March); https://euobserver.com/foreign/137170

Reuters (2016) "Britain to hire foreign trade negotiators after Brexit, says
Hammond." *Business News* (4th July); available at: http://uk.reuters.com/article/
uk-britain-eu-trade-idUKKCN0ZK0L6

Rhein, Eberhard (2012) "By 2020 the Euro zone should comprise essentially
all EU Member States." *EuroActive, plc.,* Brussels. (12th March); https://rhein.
blogactiv.eu/2012/03/12/by-2020-the-euro-zone-should-comprise-essentially-
all-eu-member-states/

Ridley, Louise (2016) "Which newspapers support Brexit in the EU
Referendum?" *Huffpost: United Kingdom* (22nd June); http://www.
huffingtonpost.co.uk/entry/which-newspapers-support-brexit_

uk_5768fad2e4b0a4f99adc6525

Ridley, Nicholas (1990) "Speaking for England." *The Spectator* (14th July), pp. 8-10

Rigby, Elizabeth; Parker, George and Peel, Quentin (2013) "Cameron races to lay ground for speech as party factions mobilise." *Financial Times* (15th January), p.6

Riley-Smith, Ben (2016a) "Cameron: Household bills to rise in event of out vote." *The Daily Telegraph* (14th May), p. 9

Riley-Smith, Ben (2016c) "Exclusive: Britain will be front of the queue for trade deal with US under Donald Trump's new Commerce Secretary." *The Telegraph* (17th December); http://www.telegraph.co.uk/news/2016/12/17/exclusive-britain-will-front-queue-trade-deal-us-donald-trumps/

Robinson, Duncan and Foy, Henry (2015) "EU to allot up to 40,000 asylum seekers in reform plan." *Financial Times* (25th May), p.5

Samuel, Henry (2014) "Migrants step up attempts to get to Britain from 'war zone' Calais." *The Daily Telegraph* (2nd September), p.13

Samuel, Henry (2015) "France gets money from Brussels to build new camp for Jungle migrants." *The Daily Telegraph* (1st September), p.13

Samuel, Henry (2016) "Gunfight in migrant camp as trafficking gangs clash." *The Daily Telegraph* (28th January), p.7

Shehab, Khan (2016) "European Parliament backs plans to create a defence union." *The Independent* (22nd November); http://www.independent.co.uk/news/world/europe/european-parliament-nato-backs-plans-create-defence-union-a7432706.html

Shipman, Tim (2014) "Bottled it? Me? Pull the other one." *The Sunday Times* (4th May), p. 19

Shipman, Tim (2015a) "EU can spend millions to back 'yes' vote." *The Sunday Times* (7th June), p.1

Shipman, Tim (2015b) "Millions of jobs 'at risk' in Brexit." *The Sunday Times* (1st November), p. 10

Shipman, Tim (2017) "Blair gets tough on migrants 13 years after opening doors." *The Sunday Times* (10th September), pp.1-2

Shipman, Tim and Evans, Peter (2016) "Travel chiefs: Brexit danger to UK tourists." *The Sunday Times* (14th February), p.1/4

Shipman, Tim, Tony Grew, and Marie Woolf (2016) "Thatcher 'would vote yes to EU'" *The Sunday Times* (7th February), p. 1

Sikka, Prem (2016) "Heard the latest Christmas story? It's about how UK banks pay all their taxes." *The Guardian* (8th December); https://www.theguardian.com/commentisfree/2016/dec/08/tax-avoidance-banks-city-london-corporation

Slack, James (2016) "David Cameron's doom-laden warning of Brexit causing war in Europe rejected by NINE in 10 voters." *Mail Online* (19th May); http://www.dailymail.co.uk/news/article-3599354/David-Cameron-s-doom-laden-warning-Brexit-causing-war-Europe-rejected-NINE-10-voters-new-polling-reveals.html

Smith, David (2016) "Britain succeeds in the EU: we'd be daft to leave it." *The Sunday Times* (22nd June), p. 4

Smith, David (2017) "Still clueless on Brexit – and it's taking a toll." *The Sunday Times* (8th October), p. 4

Speed, Barbara (2016) "What would really happen to the Calais 'jungle' camp if the UK leaves the EU?" *New Statesman* 23rd June); http://www.newstatesman.com/politics/uk/2016/06/what-would-really-happen-calais-jungle-camp-if-uk-leaves-eu

Spence, Peter (2015) "Brexit may dent UK economy, says IMF chief." *The Daily Telegraph* (12th December), p.37

Spence, Peter (2016) "Government faces worldwide hunt for trade negotiators, experts warn." *The Telegraph* (3rd July); http://www.telegraph.co.uk/business/2016/07/03/government-faces-worldwide-hunt-for-trade-negotiators-experts-wa/

Spence, Peter and Tovey, Alan (2016) "Yellen and Draghi warn of 'significant' Brexit repercussions." *The Daily Telegraph* (22nd June), p. B1

Stephens, Philip (2011) "A return to the world of Hobbes." *Financial Times* (20th October), p.8

Stewart, Heather (2017) "John Major attacks government over approach to Brexit." *The Guardian* (27th February); https://www.theguardian.com/politics/2017/feb/27/john-major-attacks-government-over-approach-to-brexit

Stone, Jon (2017) "Second EU referendum must be held on final Brexit deal, says former head of British civil service." *Independent* (21st February); http://www.independent.co.uk/news/uk/politics/brexit-second-eu-referendumformer-head-of-civil-service-lord-butler-gus-odonnell-a7592066.htm

Strange, Hannah and Crisp, James (2017) "Europe rejects calls to step in over Catalan vote violence." *The Daily Telegraph* (3rd October), p.12

Stubbington, Tommy (2017) "EU court threatens Brexit trade deals." *The Sunday Times* (14th May), p.B1

Swinford, Steven (2015) "Migrants to account for half of new homes." *The Daily Telegraph* (4th December), p.1

Swinford, Steven (2016a) "Reveal true migrant numbers, PM is told." *The Daily Telegraph* (5th March), p.1

Swinford, Steven (2016b) "We won't be bullied by foreign leaders." *The Daily Telegraph* (5th March), p.13

Swinford, Steven (2016c) "We must leave or face migrant breaking point." *The Daily Telegraph* (2nd April), p.14

Swinford, Steven (2016d) "UK 'obliged' to accept judgments of European courts, official document from ministers ahead of EU referendum reveals." *The Telegraph* (14th April); http://www.telegraph.co.uk/news/2016/04/14/uk-obliged-judgments-of-european-courts-official-document-from-m/

Swinford, Steven (2016e) "David Cameron: Brexit could lead to Europe descending into war." *The Telegraph* (9th May); http://www.telegraph.co.uk/news/2016/05/08/cameron-brexit-will-increase-risk-of-europe-descending-into-war/

Swinford, Steven (2016f) "Pensioners face a £32,000 loss from Brexit, says Osborne." *The Daily Telegraph* (27th May), p. 11

Swinford, Steven (2016g) "What will the Special Relationship look like with President Trump?" *Telegraph* (9th November) http://www.telegraph.co.uk/news/2016/11/09/what-will-the-special-relationship-look-like-under-president-don/

Swinford, Steven (2017a) "Blair's Brexit revolt insults voters, says Boris." *The Daily Telegraph* (18th February), p. 4

Swinford, Steven (2017b) "Mandelson calls for Lords to frustrate Brexit bill in Blairite plot." *The Daily Telegraph* (20th February), p. 4

Swinford, Steven (2017c) "How EU tried to hide £500,000 bill for two month's travel." *The Daily Telegraph* (10th August), pp. 4-5

Swinford, Steven (2017d) "Tory anger at officials over Brexit divorce bill." *The Daily Telegraph* (7th August), pp. 1 and 4

Swinford, Steven and Chan, Szu Ping (2016) "IMF accused of trying to 'bully

Britons into staying in the EU." *The Daily Telegraph* (14th May), p.8

Swinford, Steven and Holehouse, Matthew (2015) "Leaked memo says PM will play on dangers of Britain leaving the EU." *The Daily Telegraph,* (27th June), p. 12

Swinford, Steven and Hughes, Laura (2016) "Major is 'dismissing democracy' over Brexit says IDS." *The Daily Telegraph* (26th November), p. 8

Swinford, Steven and Watson, Leon (2017) " Boris Johnson attacks Tony Blair's 'bare-faced effrontery' after former PM urges Remainers to 'rise up' against Brexit." *The Telegraph* (17th February); http://www.telegraph.co.uk/news/2017/02/17/tony-blair-eu-brexit-mission-remainers-live/

Swinford, Steven, Josephine McKenna, and Louise Osborne (2016) " EU border warning as terrorist is found in Italy." *The Daily Telegraph* (24th December), p.1

Telegraph Reporter (2014) "Convicted Romanian burglar raped woman, 81." *The Daily Telegraph* (29th November), p.8

Telegraph Reporters (2017) "Article 50 letter: read it in full." *The Telegraph* (30th March); http://www.telegraph.co.uk/news/2017/03/29/article-50-brexit-letter-read-full/

Thatcher, Margaret (1993) *The Downing Street Years.* Harper-Collins Inc., New York

Thatcher, Margaret (2001) *On Europe.* William Collins Ltd., London

The Economist (2016a) "How to manage the migrant crisis." *The Economist* (6th February), pp.9-10

The Economist (2016b) "The Economist's guide to Britain's EU referendum" *The Economist* (15th June); https://www.economist.com/news/britain/21700592-brexit-briefs

The Economist (2016c) "Trip-wire deterrence." *The Economist* (2nd July), p. 32

The Economist (2016d) "Drawbridges up." *The Economist* (30th July), pp.16-18

The Economist (2016e) "The Tories and Brexit: mind your step." *The Economist* (8th October), pp. 27-29

The Economist (2016f) "Belgian girls aren't easy." *The Economist* (15th October), pp. 32-33

The Economist (2016g) "The age of vetocracy." *The Economist* (29th October), pp. 38

The Economist (2017a) "We will cite him in our speeches." *The Economist* (17th June), p.35

The Economist (2017b) "Have your fishcake and eat it." *The Economist* (8th

July), p.20

The Economist (2017c) "Facing up to Brexit." *The Economist* (22nd July), p.11

The Scotsman (2004) "Landlocked EU states get share of £200m fisheries hand-out" *The Scotsman* (7th May); http://www.scotsman.com/news/politics/landlocked-eu-states-get-share-of-163-200m-fisheries-hand-out-1-530018

Thomson, Adam and Stothard, Michael (2016) "Brexit touches nerve in France." *Financial Times* (2nd July), p. 9

Tisdall, Simon (2001) "Conflict looms over rapid reaction force." *The Guardian* (29th March); https://www.theguardian.com/world/2001/mar/29/worlddispatch.simontisdall

Traynor, Ian and Jowit, Juliette (2012) "A €1tn scandal or money well spent: where does the EU budget go?" *The Guardian* (22nd November); http://www.theguardian.com/world/2012/nov/21/eu-budget-battle-brussels

Treaty of Rome (1957) *The Treaty of Rome: 25th March, 1957.* Available at: http://eb.europa.eu/economy_finance/emu.../treaties/rometreaty.

UK Political Info. (2005) "2005 General election results summary." http://www.ukpolitical.info/2005.htm.

Ungoed-Thomas, Jon (2011) "The European court creeping into every area of our lives." *The Sunday Times* (13th February)

Ungoed-Thomas, and Follain, Jon (2011) "Judges with little experience on £150,000 a year." *The Sunday Times* (13th February); https://www.thetimes.co.uk/article/judges-with-little-experience-on-pound150000-a-year-9stv0sp2jqx

Ungoed-Thomas, and Leake, Jonathan (2013) "Single Dutch boat snatches a firth of England's fish quota." *The Sunday Times* (22nd December), p.17

Wagstyl, Stefan (2015) "Merkel's Bavarian ally proves a thorn in her side on refugees." *Financial Times* (8th October), p.6

Wagstyl, Stefan (2015) "Schäuble warns of refugee 'avalanche'." *Financial Times* (13th November), p.6

Wallace, Tim (2016a) "Brexit crisis? It all looks like business as usual so far." *The Daily Telegraph* (20th August), p. 29

Wallace, Tim (2016b) "Brexit offers 'large' trade opportunity, says Carney." *The Daily Telegraph* (17th September), p. 37

Wallace, Tim (2016c) "Australian negotiators arrive to begin post-Brexit trade talks." *The Telegraph* (8th October); http://www.telegraph.co.uk/business/2016/10/08/

australian-negotiators-arrive-to-begin-post-brexit-trade-talks

Wallace, Tim (2017) "UK must bring down trade deficit to avoid dangerous imbalances, warns IMF." *The Daily Telegraph* (29th July), p.33

Warner, Jeremy (2016) "Why UK must ensure survival of single market in financial services." *The Daily Telegraph* (26th September), p. 2

Warner, Jeremy (2017) "Will sterling's Brexit devaluation make the country richer or poorer?" *The Daily Telegraph* (11th January), p.2

Warrell, Helen (2013) "Influx of EU workers sparks net migration rise." *Financial Times* (29th November), p.6

Warrell, Helen and Parker, George (2015) "Migration data ominous for pro-EU camp." *Financial Times* (28th August), p.3

Waterfield, Bruno (2009a) "EU blames Georgia for starting war with Russia." *The Telegraph* (30th September); http://www.telegraph.co.uk/news/worldnews/europe/georgia/6247620/EU-blames-Georgia-for-starting-war-with-Russia.html

Waterfield, Bruno (2009b) "If Tony Blair is made President of Europe, the EU will never be the same again." *The Telegraph* (2nd October); http://www.telegraph.co.uk/news/worldnews/europe/eu/6255143/If-Tony-Blair-is-made-President-of-Europe-the-EU-will-never-be-the-same-again.html

Waterfield, Bruno (2012) "Britain refuses to sign off on EU budget." *The Telegraph* (22nd February); http://www.telegraph.co.uk/news/worldnews/europe/eu/9097659/Britain-refuses-to-sign-off-on-EU-budget.html

Waterfield, Bruno (2014a) "Get them young: Merkel plans EU education." *The Daily Telegraph* (8th March), p. 20.

Waterfield, Bruno (2014b) "Bureaucracy is crushing Europe, warns Pope." *The Daily Telegraph* (26th November), p. 15.

Watt, Holly, Claire Newell, and Ben Bryant (2014) "For sale: EU citizenship." *The Daily Telegraph* (15th March), pp. 1 and 6

Watts, Joe (2017) "Michael Hesseltine ready to defy Theresa May over Brexit ahead of Lords showdown." *The Independent* (25th February); http://www.independent.co.uk/news/uk/politics/michael-heseltine-theresa-may-brexit-house-of-lords-referendum-a7599941.html

Wheeler, Caroline (2017) "Fox wags his tail at US trade talks." *The Sunday Times* (30th July), p.12

Willsher, Kim (2002) "French head league for EU rule breaking." *The Sunday*

Telegraph (7th April), p.5

Wintour, Patrick (2014) "Tony Blair and Europe: What's he up to?" *The Guardian* (2nd June); https://www.theguardian.com/politics/2014/jun/02/tony-blair-europe-council-president-eu

Wise, Peter (2014) "'Golden visas' for Chinese investors are passport to riches for hard-up Europe." *Financial Times* (9th October), p.1

Woods, Judith (2016) "'This is another attack on women. First on our bodies, and now on our rights.'" *The Daily Telegraph* (9th January), p.16

Workman, Daniel (2017) "United Kingdom's Top Import Partners." *World's Top Exports* (27th August); http://www.worldstopexports.com/united-kingdoms-top-import-partners/

Wright, Oliver (2017) "Oppose Brexit even if that means voting for the Tories, says Blair." *The Times* (24th April), p. 11

WTO (2013) "WTO Members and Accession Candidates." *World Trade Organisation* (March); ://www.wto.org/english/thewto_e/acc_e/members_brief_e.doc

Zalan, Eszter (2016) "EU founding states pledge deeper integration." *EUObserver* (10th February), Brussels; https://euobserver.com/political/132204

Zeffman, Henry (2016) "Kinnock's on the Brussels gravy train." *The Times* (7th June), p.10

www.ingramcontent.com/pod-product-compliance
Lightning Source LLC
Chambersburg PA
CBHW031207270326
41931CB00006B/456